THE NEW COOK
COOKBOOK

Also by Raymond Sokolov:

Non-fiction
Great Recipes from The New York Times (1973)
The Saucier's Apprentice (1976)
Wayward Reporter, The Life of A. J. Liebling (1980)
Fading Feast (1981)
Why We Eat What We Eat (1991)

Fiction
Native Intelligence (1975)

THE NEW COOK
COOKBOOK

An Easy and Imaginative Guide for Getting Started in the Kitchen

Raymond Sokolov

Illustrations by Peter LaVigna

Quill/William Morrow/New York

THE NEW COOK COOKBOOK
Library of Congress Cataloging in Publication Data has been applied for.
ISBN 0-688-11141-6 (pbk.)

Printed in the United States of America

2   3   4   5   6   7   8   9   10

To My Sons

Acknowledgments

My editor, Maria Guarnaschelli, saw the need for this book, asked me to do it and encouraged me with praise and detailed, intelligent criticism as the manuscript passed piecemeal to her. My wife cheerfully endured a year of sharing me with 150 recipes and a Hewlett Packard microminicomputer. Thanks to both.

Contents

THE NEW COOK
COOKBOOK

1

BREAKING INTO THE KITCHEN

NO ONE IS BORN KNOWING HOW TO COOK. SOME FAVORED CHIL-
dren still are welcomed into the kitchen at an early age and taught
their way around food by parents. This is surely the best kind of
cooking school. But these days most of us manage to sideslip out
of the family home without learning to feed ourselves. We go to
college or take a job, move into a first apartment, and the kitchen
remains a place of mystery.

I grew up in a more or less traditional home. My mother was
a practiced and ambitious cook. From her I learned respect for food,
and she exposed me to a wide range of dishes and ingredients. She
could roast beef to a turn, bake a cherry pie and prepare far more
complicated dishes: deep-fried eggplant, sautéed sweetbreads, delicate strudels with dozens of papery layers of dough. But it never
occurred to her to show me how she did these things. And I didn't
think to ask. I was a boy; I would soon be a man. And then some
other woman would take over the job of cooking for me.

The kitchen was mother's place. Sometimes she cajoled me to
help with the dishes. Sometimes I raided the icebox. That was the
full extent of my kitchen experience, until I found myself living
in a series of dormitories, forced to put up with mystery meat,
gravity pudding and the other staple items of institutional food.

As a matter of survival, I began to buy food for myself, mainly
snacks at first, but then I met my first real cooking teacher, Spider
Groff.

Spider lived down the hall, in a room crowded with provi-
sions: tea bags, soup mix, canned sardines. He had a small arsenal
of knives and other implements. Best of all, he had a clandestine
immersion heater. Spider could boil water.

He wasn't an elegant cook, obviously, but he demystified
cooking for me, showed me I didn't need a kitchen, or fancy

equipment or training or any special background in order to get together a satisfactory meal. For him, cooking was a subversive act, a clever trick that any boy could do, like starting a fire without matches.

I hope this book will infuse the same independent, outlaw spirit in all of its readers. This is not a primer for people who are approaching the study of cuisine in a dutiful mood. It is certainly not a substitute for a complete course in all basic techniques. You will not master the art of French cooking in these pages, although you will pick up a useful battery of moves and strategies that will prepare you to make a first-rate meal for yourself and friends with a minimum of fuss, fear or folderol. You will learn to cook just about everything that is basic, from boiled eggs to roast chicken. But this is not, in the ordinary sense, a basic cookbook. It is a cookbook for beginners, but not for innocents; really it is a cookbook for opportunists, for everyone who is tired of being an outsider in the kitchen and wants a quick passport to fundamental culinary literacy.

In fact, you will end up with more than basics. There is elegance here too, and the makings of many a major dinner party, complete with pastry your mother will insist you bought. But the main purpose of this book is to launch you as a practical, bold, self-sufficient, unpretentious, Groffesque, subversive cook.

I am insisting on the word *subversive* here, because I believe that when we cook from scratch—every time we do it—we do a little bit to upset the stultifying trend abroad in the world that is rapidly turning all meals into dorm meals. Look around you. Everywhere you turn, industrially prepared food stares you in the face. A giant food industry grows and processes food on a scale unprecedented in history. Everything is provided: cake mixes, bottled dressings, frozen pizzas. Even so-called raw materials have usually been doctored. Most flour has been artificially enriched after natural nutrients have been removed. Tomatoes are hardwalled and tasteless. Fruit is picked too early to taste good, so that it will still be solid enough to travel to you from hundreds or thousands of miles away.

Most of us can't do much about the galloping evils of the basic food-supply system, except market shrewdly and buy produce, as often as possible, when it is in season locally. And we can strike a blow for good taste by avoiding prepared foods, fast foods and over-packaged foods. This is only possible if we cook for ourselves, unless, of course, we have managed to find someone else who will do the work for us. But the person who has delegated all the cooking to someone else has given away control of what he eats. It may also be that this sort of arrangement rests on the exploitation of the designated cook, but it is a certainty, even where the cook is a cheerful, enthusiastic volunteer, that the noncook is in a helpless position, much like that of the car owner who can't change a tire and has to depend on paid mechanics to keep his automobile running.

In this high-tech world, no one can be in complete charge of his life. We are all at the mercy of the schedules and competence of plumbers, television repairmen, electricians. Without making a full-time career out of learning these jobs and then doing them, it is impossible to manage a modern life entirely by yourself. And even if you did decide to become your own full-time handyman, you'd still have to continue hanging around in the waiting rooms and paying the inflated bills of doctors, lawyers, accountants and vets, unreliable and smug as they often are. You can, however, control how and what you eat to a very large extent.

The purpose of this book is to show the rank beginner the way to break into the kitchen for the first time. It will demystify cooking. It will save you money, win the admiration of friends and family, and, most important of all, it will help you to please yourself at mealtime.

The Kitchen: A User's Guide

It is possible to cook—and cook well—without a kitchen. (The next chapter will explore methods appropriate for students and other people who must make do without a stove or a refrigerator.) During the greater part of human history, and throughout all of pre-history, our species fed itself with cold food or food heated over open fires kindled afresh at each meal. If you have ever broiled a steak over a wood flame, you know that it imparts a special flavor that neither charcoal nor, certainly, an electric broiler can match. The royal kitchens of the early modern period were devoted to spit cookery, a splendid but uncertain method, which is why that great gastronomic writer Brillat-Savarin wrote, "We can learn to be cooks, but we must be born knowing how to roast."

The modern kitchen oven was invented by Benjamin Thompson of Woburn, Massachusetts, who emigrated to Europe and became a world-famous scientist under the name of Count Rumford. About 1800, he experimented with a cylindrical metal roasting oven. Rumford was generally occupied with the problem of making kitchens more thermally efficient, and with his oven he was able to save energy and, he argued, to cook better as well. To prove his point, he conducted what must have been the first modern experiment in home economics.

Rumford cut two legs of mutton of equal weight from the same carcass. Without explaining to his kitchen staff that something special was afoot, he had them roast one leg on a spit and the other in his new oven. The oven-roasted leg came out weighing 6 percent more than its spit-roasted twin. A subsequent tasting is supposed to have demonstrated that the oven produced juicier meat than the spit.

The Stove

The modern stove, despite all its clocks and chrome and see-through windows, is merely an elaboration of Count Rumford's device. It allows you to cook food under controlled conditions of temperature, inside the house, with fuels that do not take up valuable space or leave a messy residue.

The modern oven improves on Rumford's because it is thermostatically controlled, which means it has a sensing device that turns it on and off in order to maintain the heat level set on the dial. The dial does not control the amount of gas or electrical power; it controls the thermostat. All ovens run at maximum power when their thermostats let them. So there is no point in turning the dial up to 500 degrees to warm up the oven from a cold start. If the recipe you are using calls for a moderate temperature of 350 degrees, set the dial at 350. If you are using an electric oven, turn it on and wait until the electrical element, a heavy metal wire that makes a (usually visible) loop on the floor of the oven, gets red hot and then turns itself off. If the oven is in good working order, this means that it has been preheated* and that cooking should begin. The thermostat will continue to reactivate the element periodically during cooking in order to maintain a heat of 350 degrees. A similar process occurs in gas ovens. The flame falls away to a negligible level between surges.

Gas ovens, especially older models, may have to be lit by a match. Be careful when doing this. Light a long kitchen match, then apply it to the hole in the floor of the oven. Turn on the temperature dial and wait to hear the whoosh of ignited gas before setting it to its desired temperature mark. If you don't think you've lit the oven, turn off the gas, wait a minute for collected, unignited gas to disperse, and start the process from scratch. If you leave the gas on between tries, you may cause an explosion, as I did once, losing my eyelashes in the bargain.

You should also be alert to the danger of gas leaks. If you perceive a gassy smell in the kitchen, open a window immediately and call the gas company. Do not light matches. Do not turn on burners or the oven. The smell is actually a safety device. Natural gas, which is the petroleum byproduct supplied to kitchens through pipes by utility companies, is naturally odorless, but the manufacturer adds a chemical odor so that you can detect leaks. This odor is perceptible with some ovens just after you light them. It dis-

---

*Preheating is a barbarism as objectionable as the airlines' cant expression preboarding, but we seem to be stuck with both words.

perses rapidly if the oven is running properly.

Most ovens can be set to run across a range of temperatures from 200 to 500 degrees. A "slow" oven runs at 300 or below; a "moderate" oven runs at 350; a "fast" oven runs at 400 or above. Recipes almost always give an indication of the right oven temperature. When in doubt, set the temperature at 350 and check to see what is happening to the food. You can't readjust oven temperatures rapidly with the dial, but you can radically affect what is going on by leaving the door open for a bit while the heat readjusts, or by putting a metal baking pan between the heat source and the food.

The French chef and cooking teacher Jacques Pepin was an apprentice in a restaurant in Bourg-en-Bresse, where ovens were in use throughout the day to cook a wide variety of dishes. These ovens ran at full force at all times. The cooks coped by placing food higher or lower in the oven and by shielding them with metal sheets. Most home cooks do not have to bother with such problems, but it is a good idea to remember that oven temperature is always a thermostatically arrived at compromise. And in old ovens the insulation packed inside the oven door may have settled and left a heat leak, which will make the oven unreliable and erratic. If you suspect this has happened to your oven, the first thing to do is to buy an oven thermometer to check things out scientifically. The next thing to do is to improvise as above. Uncontrollably fast ovens will not work for meringues and other foods that require gentle temperatures. They will cook most things perfectly well, however, if you just take a look at the food from time to time. Remember that cooking is not a delicate, complex activity. You are not building a nuclear reactor. Common sense will take you very far at the stove.

For instance, your mother wit should be enough to tell you that the different levels in the oven give you the chance to move food away from the full intensity of the heat source. Most foods should be positioned at the middle level of the oven. If you are forced to cook two or more dishes at the same time in the same oven, there is no problem if everything is meant to cook at the same temperature and if all the food fits on the same rack. If the dishes require different temperatures, put the food that should cook at a slower heat above the food that should cook at a faster heat. If everything requires the same heat (which is likely, since 350 is far and away the most common oven temperature), and you can't fit it all on one rack, just remember that the food on the higher level will cook at a slower rate than the recipe predicts. Expect trouble if you stack delicate concoctions such as soufflés and puff pastries in crowded ovens.

Remember too that the wire racks that come with your oven are very good heat conductors. Always use a potholder to move them once preheating has occurred. And if you are cooking a pie or some other pastry, put a baking sheet or pan on the rack during the preheating period so that the heat of the rack will be dispersed evenly and won't create hot spots that will distort the baking process. It is also a good idea to set a metal baking pan lined with aluminum foil under dishes that are likely to bubble up and overflow during baking. You can throw away the foil instead of laboriously cleaning the oven bottom. This is the most dismal task I know. Some (expensive) electric ranges are self-cleaning. They can be set to run at a very high heat that incinerates baked-on food from the oven walls. It accumulates in a convenient pile of ash and can be swept away. Watch out, though, because self-cleaning ovens are made to lock shut until they return to room temperature. This protects you from burning yourself by accidentally opening the oven when it is dangerously hot.

I once attended a dinner party where the hostess, anxious that her gleaming chrome oven was leaking heat through the door and not cooking a pork roast fast enough, threw on the self-cleaning lock and then couldn't open the door. We sat there while she cut the power in the house in a desperate attempt to remove her trapped roast. Two hours later the lock gave up, and the roast emerged, blackened and dry.

Some gas ovens are "continuous cleaning." They also pulverize accumulated food by running hot, but they do not do the complete job.

For most ovens, however, the cook is the cleaner. So the best thing to do is prepare for the inevitable by placing a layer of aluminum foil on the bottom of the oven. Set it under the electrical element (or, in a gas oven, poke a hole through it just over the hole where you light the gas). It can be thrown away from time to time, and it will catch most of the spills. Still, some food juices will vaporize and attach themselves to the walls of the oven. There are various commercial oven cleaners—noxious, caustic chemicals that can be applied to oven surfaces to eat away persistent accumulations. I cannot make myself do this more than twice a year, but it has to be done sometime if you want your oven to function properly over its full lifetime.

Like Coke machines, few ovens are the same. They range, as it were, from the narrow, flimsy models preferred by cheap-jack apartment landlords—"real estate ranges"—to massive commercial ovens built for restaurants. If you are tempted to buy a restaurant range, remember that it produces huge amounts of heat and should be vented directly to the outdoors, a very costly thing to do. And since a restaurant range is made from much heavier sheet metal than a normal stove, it will take much more energy to preheat. On the other hand, it will last longer and its more powerful burners will boil large quantities of liquid faster.

For most of us, however, a conventional range is a better choice. Choose one without clocks, timers and other gadgets that will stop running before you know it. They are of little use when they do run, and they increase the cost of the range appreciably, like extras on a car. Do, however, consider three really important factors:

1. Gas versus electric. Despite many improvements in electric stove tops, they are still greatly inferior to gas burners. Electric burners do not spring instantly to high heat. They cannot be reduced to a flicker at the flick of a dial. Gas is instantaneously controllable, across the entire heat range. Cooking on electric burners means that you have to calculate in advance which levels of heat you are going to need, and then turn on several burners so that you can move the food back and forth as the recipe requires. Even then it is difficult to know exactly what effect a particular burner

speed will have on a particular pot that contains a particular volume of food, and awkward last-minute adjustments may be necessary. Add to that the possibility that you may want to cook many things at the same time, filling all your burners and preventing easy access to a burner running at the temperature you want when you want it. Furthermore, electric ranges require 220-volt wiring, an expensive and usually impossible retrofit for older apartment buildings. This is why most of New York City cooks with gas.

Gas burners have only two defects, and they are minor. A careless person could conceivably leave an unlit burner running and fill the kitchen with explosive gas, or a leaking connection could also imperil your safety. Millions of people do, nevertheless, manage to avoid blowing themselves up every day of the year. Second, an unventilated gas range deposits an unappealing film of grease on kitchen surfaces. People with gas ranges have to clean their kitchens from top to bottom fairly often, unless they have an exhaust fan running in a hood over the stove.

Gas ovens, on the other hand, are not better than electric ovens. Some people say they are less sensitive. Perhaps the best of both worlds includes a free-standing gas stove top and an electric wall oven.

2. Or do I mean two ovens? This is a question the individual will have to work out for himself. In my case, life goes on quite well with only one oven. I rarely do the kind of volume cooking that is convenient only with a second oven. If, however, you have the space and the money for two ovens, don't hesitate to install them. But I know practically no one who really uses a second oven except at Thanksgiving and Christmas, when a turkey fills one oven and they need space for pumpkin pies. The sensible cook with only one oven will get around this by baking the pies the night before.

3. Finally, you will want to consider how many burners you need and how close together they should be. For most people (quantity cooks once again excepted), the conventional four burners should suffice, amply. But pick a stove that clusters them fairly close together, so that when you want to boil stock or soup for a multitude in a very large pot, you can apply the heat from all the burners.

Riding the Range

You may have always wondered, but been afraid to ask, why some dishes are cooked in ovens and some are cooked on top of the stove. There is no mystery here, and the sensible person can decide which heat source to use, in most cases, without consulting a cookbook. It comes to this: Almost everything except cakes, pastries, and other fragile desserts can be cooked on top of the stove, over direct heat, if you are careful and/or you use a substantial enough pot to shield large or delicate quantities of food from the heat to prevent burning. Think of pot roast—the big pot with its liquid medium distributes heat to the meat and acts like a minioven.

Still and all, for large roasts and birds and fish, the oven is the cooking venue of choice. Its slow, indirect heat will cook big things thoroughly, without constant attention. It also allows you to cook roasts with the dry heat they require. The oven is virtually essential for delicate foods that insist on even heat: pastries, breads, soufflés, meringues. Finally, there are dishes that can be done over a burner or in the oven, but which are simpler and safer in the oven, such as certain stews and braised meats—foods in liquid mediums that shouldn't boil and that would require lots of attention on top of the stove, but which purr away happily for hours in the oven. You will get a feel for this category of cooking as time goes on. But, in general, remember that big and dry or delicate foods prosper in the oven, basking in its unaggressive warmth.

Some foods, on the other hand, can't be cooked on top of the stove or in the oven. They must be exposed to direct heat, but the stove burners won't help because of the law of gravity. If, for instance, you want to broil a steak indoors, you will need to sear the meat directly. Now you could hold the steak over a burner, but this would be tedious and meat juices would make the burner sputter and smoke. Or, if you wanted to melt grated cheese sprinkled over a dish after it had been otherwise fully cooked, you couldn't do it over a burner because the heat comes from below, but the oven would take too long.

That is why God created broilers, which are nothing more than sources of direct overhead heat. They come in three varieties:

1. Most electric ovens have a second heating element located on their ceiling. You turn the dial to the broil setting and this upper element goes on. You can control its heat in the same way that you would control the heat of the lower element. But the manufacturer will have provided a special broil setting on the temperature dial. This overrides the thermostat and keeps the element running without pause. As a result, the heat is constant—and high. You control the intensity of the broiling by moving the food closer or farther from the element, by raising or lowering the rack.

2. In gas stoves, typically, the broiler is a separate compartment located underneath the oven. It has its own door and a sliding rack with a pan set into it. The heating unit is the same large, long gas burner that fires the oven. But food put in the broiler is directly exposed to heat from above. As with electric stoves, the temperature dial that controls the oven's heat has a broil setting, which overrides the thermostat and forces the burner to run constantly. Here again, the cook controls the speed and intensity of broiling by deciding how close to bring the food to the heat source. Gas broilers tend to be fairly shallow, and this limits the size of food they can handle.

3. Eye-level broilers, by and large, operate the same way as other broilers. They are, as their name implies, hung at eye level, usually just above the burner area. Some people think they are a hazard, because food can spatter out into an unwary person's eyes. I think this is an exaggerated danger, and eye-level broilers do have the advantage of running on separate heating units, so that the oven can be run simultaneously at a different temperature. Of course, this convenience runs up the cost of the stove, and most of us do not often require this flexibility.

This by no means exhausts all existing types of kitchen heat sources. But anyone who needs to know about salamanders, microwave ovens and convection ovens has already gone beyond the scope of this book. At any rate, I have been cooking for more than twenty years, and I have rarely, if ever, felt the need for these tools.

Keeping Cool

The refrigerator-freezer is also not strictly necessary for most cooking, but it certainly helps, especially in summer and in the overheated environments many of us inhabit in the winter. Few readers can possibly be entirely naïve about refrigerators. I am the only American I know who has spent a year in a household without one (as a Fulbright student in Oxford, England, 1963). This experience made me see how overly dependent I had been on refrigeration. Like many Americans, I had had a horror of leaving food in contact with the open air. Of course, cold retards spoilage, but the best refrigerator cannot prevent spoilage altogether. Even freezers do not eliminate change completely. Over time, flavors degrade, colors change. Freezing seriously damages berries and other foods with waterfilled cells that burst when frozen.

I have always made do with the refrigerators already present in the various places I have lived over the years. The only one I ever bought was a much-used Norge, a "prewar box" my college roommate and I acquired in the fall of 1959 from a landlord renovating an apartment building. It functioned nobly for the next four years, at which point we sold it at a profit to younger students.

In those days, you could judge a person's moral worth by measuring the depth of rime accumulated on the metal surface of the small internal freezing unit located inside the main refrigeration compartment of his icebox. Householders of dubious character let the ice pile up. Serious folk defrosted early and often. A young woman for whom I had a yen refused my invitation to lunch because, she said, she had to spend the afternoon defrosting her refrigerator. This announcement caused my yen to abate. It was hard to stay interested in someone who just turned off the machine, left the door open and let room temperature take its course. At the other extreme were those who pampered themselves with electric heaters that hurried the process along. Real men and women boiled water in the largest pot that would fit inside a closed freezing compartment. In a few minutes this loosened the ice from the compartment's walls, and the blade of a metal spatula would pry away the frost in sheets.

Since that time, refrigerator design has moved forward, eliminating manual defrosting from the burden of human drudgery but complicating our lives with an expensive array of gadgets. Does anyone really need automatic ice machines or ice-water dispensers? Why would anyone pay extra for a side-by-side refrigerator-freezer when many cheaper horizontally divided machines put the less frequently opened freezer unit underneath and thereby reduce stooping?

There are only four other things worth saying here about refrigerators. First, they should be kept well organized and inventoried. Otherwise, you will lose valuable edibles in the general chaos and waste time rummaging and remarketing for ingredients you already have. Second, wrap or package as much food as you can. Icebox odor ruins food. Plastic containers are worth the trouble. Third, be sure the refrigerator is really refrigerating. If it won't hold an internal ambient temperature of below 45 degrees Fahrenheit; call the repairman. Freezers should stay colder than 0 degrees Fahrenheit; otherwise they aren't going to preserve food safely. Fourth, keep the refrigerator and its freezer full. Solid objects retain cold better than air. A full refrigerator is, therefore, cheaper to run. And the refrigerator is probably more expensive to operate than any other appliance in the home except an air-conditioner.

Pots, Pans, Etc.

Thanks to the ingenuity and avarice of kitchenware manufacturers, there is no end to this subject. A few years ago, a team of highly intelligent experts spent months and months and thousands of dollars testing virtually every utensil on the market in order to produce a comprehensive guide. They scrutinized salometers and larding needles as well as more mundane objects such as sieves. The resulting book, *The Cooks' Catalogue,* was a success and, although the market has moved on, may still be useful to folks hell-bent on outfitting their kitchens to the nines. This is obviously not the approach a neophyte in matters culinary ought to take. At the other extreme, it might theoretically be useful to start with cheap, thin pots and dull stainless-steel knives from the five-and-dime so that you could see why shoddy equipment is no bargain. An experienced cook can cope with paper-thin aluminum pots that burn food in a trice, but a beginner should not have to worry about such problems. Someone starting out in the kitchen ought to buy good, practical equipment, piece by piece, as it's needed.

Better equipment does cost more than junk, but not that much more. As Julia Child points out in *Mastering the Art of French Cooking:* "A big enameled-iron casserole costs no more than a 6-rib roast . . . a large enameled skillet can be bought for the price of a leg of lamb . . . a fine paring knife may cost less than two small lamb chops."

And, of course, pots last for many meals. Cheap ones last almost as long as good ones; and because they have to be stored, they will tempt you not to replace them with better ones.

So find out where the restaurant-supply outlets are near you. Their prices are generally lower than cookware boutiques with French names. Restaurant-supply stores also tend to stock heavy-gauge cast-aluminum pots. They are the most economical way to go. Eventually, these homely but sturdy and practical pots will pit; they discolor slightly in use as well. But for many years they will give good, if unglamorous, service, conducting heat evenly through their heavy bottoms to the food you cook. Get several sizes of saucepans. You will also need a large stockpot, not only for stock, but for cooking pasta and boiling lobsters. An eight-quart pot is fine to begin with. You should probably also have a stockpot at least twice that large for feeding crowds.

Everyone needs at least one skillet. Actually, everyone needs three or four, in diameters ranging from six to eighteen inches. Heavy cast iron is the material of choice—cheap and efficient. I know, I know, iron and aluminum react with white wine and eggs and discolor the food they contain. That is why you should eventually acquire a pot and a skillet whose cooking surfaces are enamel, stainless steel, tinned copper or a synthetic nonstick material. But there is time for this. You can probably get quite far along with two sturdy saucepans and a skillet, for top-of-the-stove recipes.

For the oven, you can get away with truly shoddy equipment, because the heat is not direct. Almost any kind of roasting pan will do. So will dime-store cookie sheets, jelly-roll pans, pie pans and cake tins. For oven braising, however, it will pay to invest in an enameled-iron casserole, which can also go directly on a burner and looks good enough to present at the table.

Knives

Don't try to save money here. One of the most insidious cons in modern industrial life is the cheap stainless-steel knife, especially the kind that curves up like a scimitar at the end, the better to puncture your palm with when you try to rock it in the classic chopping maneuver (about which more later). There is one exception to this dictum: Top-of-the-line stainless-steel serrated bread knives work fine and seem to hold their edge. But for active slicing and chopping, you need a blade that can be easily resharpened. You can do very nicely with two first-rate carbon-steel knives—a big chef's knife and a small paring knife. Carbon steel is not stainless. It will rust overnight if left sitting around all wet in the kitchen. It discolors under the best of circumstances. But if you exercise reasonable care to scour and dry carbon-steel knives, you will get the best possible results. There are serviceable stainless-steel-alloy knives on the market, but I have never been able to get them as sharp as I'd like.

The reason for this is that carbon steel is relatively soft, compared to stainless, and it can, therefore, be easily sharpened. Just keep one of those new, harder-than-diamond, ceramic sharpening devices (the Zip-Zap or its equivalent) by your cutting board and use it often. Don't waste your money on an old-fashioned sharpening steel, the rod that you've seen paired with a useless stainless-steel knife in fancy carving sets.

Gadgets

No one can own too many wooden spoons, rubber spatulas for scraping food out of bowls, slotted spoons, metal spatulas, ladles, vegetable peelers, wire whisks. You will soon have drawers full of them. Buy them as you feel the need.

Do not buy an electric can opener or a manual can opener that attaches to the wall. The first is a waste of money. The second is almost always hard to maneuver because it is cramped up against the wall. Instead, look for the cheap portable can opener, sold everywhere, that has two handles covered with plastic. There is a really cheap version of this gadget, but it doesn't work nearly as well and will hurt your hands because its arms are bare metal.

Wooden cutting boards are essential. Harder surfaces damage knives. Knives damage wooden counters. Besides, cutting boards double in brass as serving trays for nondrip foods.

Blenders, Mixers and Processors

These days you can probably do without a blender. The food processor will do everything a blender can do, more conveniently and reliably, except for fine pureeing. Unless you insist on a baby-food texture to soups, save your money. If you do buy a blender, don't get sucked into springing for a flashy model with many buttons. The machine has only two speeds, fast or slow, no matter how many buttons the manufacturer has stuck on to amaze the innocent.

Blenders work best when they are attacking cold semiliquid or liquid foods. Their motors are not mighty and their blades are small and easily clogged. Therefore, blend dry foods in small batches, or add water to them where possible. Do not attempt to blend a hot mixture. The blades release steam explosively and cause a scalding eruption from the jar. I did this once during a rushed television demonstration and had to pretend I hadn't suffered a second-degree burn because thousands of book buyers were out there watching. If you must blend hot food, blend only small batches, turning the motor on and off in quick alternation, so that steam is released without turning the blender into a mini-Vesuvius.

When chopping nuts in a blender you should also use small batches and flip the switch off and on, so that the nuts don't release excessive oil and turn to nut butter in the blender jar.

At any rate, the processor is the tool of preference for this task, as it is for so many jobs that require cutting, slicing or chopping. When James Beard, the father of us all in the food field, acquired his first processor, he said it was like having another person in the kitchen. Myself, I can see the point of the processor if you are frequently involved with repetitive jobs and fairly large quantities of food, but you really ought to learn to do the basic culinary techniques by hand, to get the feel of the way foods react to the basic processes, before you turn those jobs over to a machine. And if the cost of a processor makes you cringe even slightly, wait for a while before you buy one.

The same is true of electric mixers. I will not try to tell you that the powerful machines sold in good kitchenware stores will not beat egg whites to the same air-filled volume that an experienced cook with a strong wrist can achieve with a balloon whisk, because I think they can. I also think that it is far cheaper and more instructive to make your debuts with a whisk. It will do an admirable job with egg whites and yolks. It will also whip heavy cream. If you just can't stand the effort, a portable electric mixer will do almost as well as a whisk, and it will equal the big machines in everything but power.

Measurement

We are the descendants of pioneers, and that is why we measure by volume instead of by weight, like the rest of the world. Early settlers didn't have scales, they made do with cups and spoons. This is what Americans still do, although we now use standardized cups and measuring spoons. However, this is still an inferior method because it is less convenient and less accurate than weighing out ingredients on a kitchen scale. Flour, for instance, settles in a bag and may require sifting if it is to be accurately measured in a cup. Eggs come in different sizes. Nuts are not uniform and pack differently in a cup. Individual cooks will load tablespoons differently. How much whole fresh parsley should you start with to produce a (level?) tablespoon of finely chopped parsley?

Such quandaries and many others vanish when you use a scale. But this is America and you will be using American cookbooks with recipes written for volumetrically arrived at quantities. So this book measures by volume, except when ingredients are conventionally sold by weight. You should still get a kitchen scale, because some recipes are easier to do if you can weigh the ingredients, and you can also use a scale to check your butcher from time to time.

The standard American measuring cup holds 8 liquid ounces. It is the equivalent of ½ pint. Two cups equal 1 pint. Four cups make 1 quart.

That was easy, but the rest isn't and should be memorized when you have nothing better to do—for instance, when you are waiting in line at the bank.

One cup equals 16 tablespoons. One tablespoon equals 3 teaspoons.

Measuring spoons usually come in groups of four: tablespoon, teaspoon, ½ teaspoon, and ¼ teaspoon.

Test yourself. Quickly now: How many tablespoons in ¼ cup? How would you measure out ½ tablespoon?

This kind of thing will soon become automatic. And, as you

gain confidence in cooking, you will see that, except when baking, hyperexact measurement is not essential to good results. For the moment, however, it is a good idea to leave nothing to chance. Level the tops of measuring spoons with the back of a knife to make sure you have the quantity specified in the recipe. Don't improvise with regular spoons and cups. Most teacups hold only 6 ounces. Flatware teaspoons are not necessarily the same size as measuring teaspoons.

Recipes

Modern recipes have a special grammar that no one bothers to explain. They begin with a list of ingredients presented in the order of their first appearance in the recipe, like characters in a dramatis personae. In a standard recipe, each ingredient is also listed in the form that it will be used in the body of the recipe. For example, a well-written recipe might list:

1 medium onion, peeled and finely chopped.

This is to help the cook prepare for action. The experienced reader of recipes will scan the ingredients list at least twice before starting to cook. The first time is to make sure every ingredient is available in the house. The second time is to see if any prep work is necessary before actually launching into the recipe proper.

A good ingredient list should also explain in a concise manner how to buy unusual ingredients—how to identify them and where to locate them. Sometimes the ingredient list will refer you to a note if a particular ingredient requires extensive explanation. For example:

1 piece galanga or galingale (see note)

The note will tell where Asian spices such as galanga are obtainable.

Normally, the way an ingredient is presented follows a standard format. The quantity required for the entire recipe comes first, then the name of the ingredient. Any prep work is mentioned after a comma. For example:

1 pound potatoes, peeled and diced (about 4 cups)

The reason for the parenthetical quantity is to reassure the reader without a scale who bought potatoes a while ago in a five-pound bag and isn't really sure how many will make a pound. The instruction implies that the careful person will measure as he or she dices each potato. Of course, a kitchen scale would eliminate the need for this fussing, but the writer of the recipe can't expect most readers to have scales. Perhaps it would have been better to write: 4 peeled and diced medium potatoes (about 4 cups).

Prep directions can also be written in ahead of the name of the ingredient, but this implies that the measurement is done after the prep work. For example:

4 cups chopped onion

Or:

4 filleted trout

In the second example the writer assumes that most people will be buying the trout from a fish market and will be starting out with filleted fish. If weight were important, it could be inserted as follows:

4 filleted trout (about 6–8 ounces each)

Or, perhaps more usefully:

4 10–12-ounce trout, filleted

This implies that the trout weighed 10–12 ounces as whole fish, before the fish man cleaned them. Since some stores sell fish according to their uncleaned weight and others sell them already filleted, the recipe should probably indicate both weights. For example:

> 4 10–12-ounce trout, filleted (they should then weigh 6–8 ounces)

Sometimes ingredients are listed without quantities or weight. For example:

> **Salt**
>
> *Or:*
>
> **Oil**

Note that these "naked" ingredients are capitalized. This is usually done to indicate that the cook will have to exercise taste or discretion in deciding how much of the ingredient is required, how much salt will please those eating the dish or how much oil will just barely coat the bottom of the particular skillet the cook is actually using.

In general, as you translate recipes into real-life cooking, remember these three tactics:

1. Not all recipes are written grammatically. It is always a good idea to check the full recipe to see that all ingredients are listed at the top. Nothing is more frustrating than to come across a mystery ingredient lurking in a direction you hadn't bothered to read (and which the author hadn't bothered to mention in the ingredient list).

2. You can eliminate other unpleasant surprises and plan your work time better if you read the full recipe and try to imagine what you will have to do and when and with what utensils.

3. Finally, if you are cooking more than one dish at a time, you will have to consider how to coordinate all the steps from all the recipes concurrently and how to intersperse these steps so that your equipment can accommodate everything. This is hard to do when you haven't cooked much and can't really look at four recipes and picture how a whole meal will unfold.

Shopping

You can't cook what you can't buy. If no market near you is selling fresh raspberries, you will have to decide whether you can get by with frozen. If they don't sell monkfish in your neighborhood, you'll have to do without or trek to a specialty fishmonger farther afield.

In providing ingredients for your kitchen, you must take what the seasons, the supermarket chains and the elite purveyors provide. Every locality is different, obviously, but some general principles apply everywhere:

1. Keep yourself informed of what is in the market. Plan menus around ingredients that look and smell fresh, and that are attractively priced. The practiced cook should plan a meal in the market, not at home with a cookbook in hand.

2. Shop often. Laying away food for a week may be convenient, but it makes for stale food and discourages you from impulsive, creative thinking about meals.

3. Eliminate all canned vegetables (except beets and Italian tomatoes) from your shopping list.

4. Buy staples in quantity—rice, sugar, flour—and store in tight containers.

5. Patronize specialists for perishable items. Greengrocers and fishmongers are bound to do a better job with lettuce or bass than giant chainstores.

6. Avoid baked goods, the most labor-intensive, overpriced and poorest quality items in most markets. Bake for yourself or eat fruit.

7. Avoid bread that sinks under the weight of your hand.

8. Free-standing butcher shops are usually worth an extra stop. They cut the meat for you, to suit your needs. They don't pre-package meat in deceptively priced plastic packages. Good butchers have helpful ideas about cuts of meat you might not be familiar with. They can special-order cuts they don't have immediately on hand. They have marrow bones. They give credit.

9. Fresh fish look fresh, smell clean and have bright eyes.

10. Picking fruits and vegetables at their peak is a skill learned over a lifetime, but here are a few basic tips: Good melons are fragrant; the best strawberries are always on the top layer in the box; the best, most reliably ripe pineapples come from Hawaii; apples with names you don't recognize are almost always tastier than mass-produced varieties you know about; pears are usually sold slightly hard and need a day or two of ripening at room temperature; apricots sold east of Denver are almost always disappointingly tasteless, because they were picked green in the West so they could survive long-distance shipment.

11. Buy only locally produced, vine-ripened tomatoes. For cooking, use canned Italian tomatoes when fresh local tomatoes are out of season.

12. Inspect all egg crates for broken eggs. Roll each egg to make sure it isn't cracked underneath (if an egg sticks, it has leaked through a crack in the shell).

13. Check labels of dairy products for expiration dates.

14. Buy unsalted butter, when it is on special, and freeze until needed.

15. Buy only fresh American lamb. It tastes better than frozen lamb from New Zealand.

16. Caveat emptor.

Keeping Clean for Cuisine

The single most important rule of efficient, successful cooking is to clean up the kitchen while you cook. Waiting until the end is pure folly. The work space is cluttered, ingredients contaminate each other. Dessert tastes of garlic. And quickly there is not even space to wash properly.

I shall assume I don't need to discuss the techniques of normal dishwashing. But it may be worthwhile to consider the maintenance of pots and pans.

In addition to a standard dishwashing liquid, I keep a sponge, a Brillo pad, a Rescue pad and a Chore Boy copper-mesh pad near my sink. The Chore Boy pulls away large accretions of food; the Brillo attacks smoother encrustations. These aggressive pads cannot be used on scratchable copper or other surfaces they will mark permanently. Enter Rescue, a milder abrasive. And for even more delicate surfaces, use a sponge or one of the pads designed for scouring nonstick surfaces.

Soak heavily encrusted pots in soapy hot water. If all else fails, apply oven cleaner.

The Game Plan

Don't look for an introductory section on basic techniques in this book. Detailed explanations of culinary terms and operations are given in the main text, whenever a new technique is first mentioned. As a result, this book might be called front-loaded. Its earlier recipes are sometimes elaborately filled with detailed explanations. Later ones are more concise but refer back to earlier explanations. There is also an index, which will refer you to explanations of basic procedures in the main text. So start anywhere you like. Cook what appeals to you first. You're in charge.

2

IN
MY ROOM

THE EASIEST WAY TO BEGIN COOKING IS NOT TO COOK AT ALL. Recipes that don't require a stove—or any heat source for that matter—turn out to be among the most useful food ideas for someone starting out as a cook. They teach basic techniques of ingredient preparation. They can be executed almost anywhere: in a dormitory room or on an office desktop. And they include dishes that lend themselves to a wide variety of entertaining, most especially for cocktail parties or other informal gatherings. Dips, hors d'oeuvres, cold main dishes, salads and desserts can all be done without cooking, and without making any concessions to elegance or sophistication.

One of the most celebrated cooks in New York, a frequent subject of articles in *The Times,* first broke into print because of her elaborate tables of appetizers, many of them uncooked. Raw food is also an important feature of the *nouvelle cuisine* menus in up-to-date restaurants.

Almost everyone has some experience with no-stove cooking. And it seems unnecessary to provide instructions for assembling sandwiches from cold cuts or serving fruit per se, but I have provided some suggestions for interesting fruit dishes that go one step beyond passing a bowl and for main dishes that are a step above ham and cheese in complexity.

I have stopped short, however, at Japanese raw fish, since I have never yet encountered a nonprofessional capable of the exquisite knife work that lies at the heart of good sushi and sashimi.

Finally, because so many of the dishes I have included are ideal companions for cocktails, this chapter ends with a few classic drink recipes, some of them equally good without alcohol, and a practical introduction to wine.

Dips and Beyond

Guacamole

This is the peppy avocado puree that dates back to Aztec days in Mexico and is now familiar to almost every living American. The basic recipe is very simple. Canned green *chiles serranos* are now available in almost any large supermarket. Tostados, crunchy fried tortilla wedges usually called taco chips, have almost replaced the potato chip.

> 1 small onion
> 1 or 2 *chiles serranos* (small green hot peppers always available canned, but use fresh ones if you can find them in a specialty store; wash hands thoroughly after touching)
> 1 large or 2 small very ripe avocados
> 3 canned Italian tomatoes (8 ounces total)
> Salt

1. Slice the root end and the top off the onion. This makes it easy to peel off the skin. Then cut in half. Put one half in the blender. Chop the other half finely: Put the onion on the cutting board with the flat (sliced) side down. Slice thinly, straight up and down. Reassemble the slices. Rotate 90 degrees. Slice again. Now, holding the onion together, flip it up so that it is standing on its side. Slice again. With each slice, small, fairly regular little onion cubes should fall from the knife. (This same three-dimensional slicing process is how onions are always chopped, except that when you start with a whole onion, you set it down first on its root end, make two sets of perpendicular slices and then turn it on its side for the last set of slices.) Reserve the chopped onion.

2. Add the chile(s) to the reserved half-onion in the blender and puree.

3. If the avocado is truly ripe, you should be able to peel it just by squeezing the skin until it pulls away. Otherwise, cut it in half, remove the large pit and scoop out the yellow flesh. Put it in a bowl and mash it with a wooden spoon. Work in the onion-chile paste.

4. Slice the tomatoes in half. Scoop out the seeds and discard. Then keep slicing until you have cut them into small cubes. Stir into the avocado puree along with the reserved chopped onion. Add salt to taste. Serve right away.

Mayonnaise

The best and most important of all cold sauces is very easy to make from scratch. Handmade mayonnaise is a luxurious vehicle for a vast spectrum of flavors. It is also nothing like store-bought mayo, which is not loathsome, just different and not sublime like the real thing. Real mayonnaise is nothing more than an egg yolk coaxed into accepting as much oil as it can. (By oil, I mean some form of vegetable oil of the sort usually extracted from olives, corn or peanuts.) The result is voluptuous and golden.

Unfortunately, there is a false rumor going around that making mayonnaise yourself requires the skill of a master chemist: Add a smidgen too much oil to the egg yolk and you've irrevocably curdled the whole ultrasensitive emulsion. This can happen, but it is easy to avoid and almost as easy to fix.

Mayonnaise is especially easy to make if you put in a small amount of mustard at the beginning. This is not absolutely classic, but it has plenty of tradition behind it. The mustard (preferably a mild Dijon type) helps to hold the sauce together during the first crucial moments. Unless you particularly want the flavor of olive oil in your mayonnaise, you may as well join most French cooks in using essentially flavorless peanut oil. Corn oil is fine too, and cheaper in this country. In the recipe below, as in all the recipes in this book, the egg called for is a "large"egg. This does not mean you should go hunting for a giant egg. Large is an official size grading that you will find marked on egg cartons in the market. Large eggs are, in fact, smaller than extra-large eggs and much smaller than jumbos.

> 1 **large egg**
> 1 **teaspoon wine vinegar or lemon juice**
>   **Salt**
>   **Pepper**
> 1 **teaspoon Dijon-type mustard**
> 1 **cup oil, approximately**

1. Cracking the egg: Get out two small bowls—one to catch the egg white, one for the yolk. (This recipe doesn't use the white, but you should save it if you have access to a freezer. Frozen egg whites store well for weeks at a time in a sealed plastic container. Once you've established an egg-white cache, you can keep adding more egg whites to it as you collect them, and when you have a dozen—keep a tally on a piece of paper taped to the container—make **angel food cake** as described on page 84.) Crack the egg by holding it in one hand and rapping it sharply but not violently against the side of a bowl. Try to produce the crack somewhere near the middle of the egg so that you end up with two more-or-less-equal eggshell halves. This makes the next part easier.

2. Separating the egg: Work your thumbs into the crack in the eggshell and pull the shell open, turning your palms upward, so that the contents are contained in both halves without spilling out. Be prepared for some egg white to spill out as you crack open the egg. This is no problem as long as you have positioned the egg over the bowl where you intend to collect the egg whites. Do not allow the egg yolk to fall out into this bowl. Instead, pass the yolk back and forth between the two shell halves, until all or almost all of the white has dripped into the egg-white bowl. Now drop the yolk into the other bowl. It doesn't matter if it smashes when it hits the bowl.

3. Now add the vinegar or lemon juice, salt, pepper and mus-

tard to the yolk. Note that no quantity is given for the salt and pepper. This means that you are being asked to decide for yourself how much to put in. This is what old-fashioned recipes mean when they tell you to add salt "to taste" or to "correct seasoning." Since you have been putting salt and pepper on food all your life, you should have some idea of how much you will need in order to flavor an egg yolk and a cup of oil, but to be safe, go easy at this stage. Start with ½ teaspoon of salt and 3 or 4 turns of the pepper mill. You can add more at the end. It's just easier to do at this stage, but don't worry, you are quite unlikely to overseason a batch of mayonnaise. (This is also probably the moment to say that *pepper* here and henceforth means freshly ground whole black peppercorns, ground by you from a mill. It tastes better.)

4. Beat the yolk together with the other ingredients in the bowl. It's easiest to do this with a medium-size wire whisk. You can also use a rubber spatula or a wooden spoon. All three of these implements are highly useful and cheap. Whichever you use, work the yolk mixture until it is smooth and uniform. This takes only a few seconds.

5. Measure out the oil. The best way is to pour it into a glass measuring cup with a pouring spout. Then begin dribbling the oil into the yolk mixture, beating it in as you pour. This is the critical moment. If you put more than a few drops in at the beginning, the mayonnaise won't take and the oil will just sit there in pools on the yolk mixture. After you've made mayonnaise a few times, you'll be able to pour in the oil in a steady stream and whisk it in fast enough to prevent trouble. But for now, I suggest pouring in a small amount, then beating it in completely, then pouring in some more oil. After you've worked in, say, a quarter of the oil, you should notice that the mixture has thickened and changed. You can now pour the oil more rapidly. But keep beating it as before. The mayonnaise should be quite stiff by the time you've incorporated all the oil. If for some reason the mayonnaise curdles and separates, vigorously beat in a small amount of mustard, which should bring it back.

6. To store, stir a tablespoon of boiling water into the may-

onnaise. This sets it and keeps it from separating in the refrigerator, where it should be kept in a tightly sealed jar.

You now have an extremely versatile medium to work with. Aside from more salt or pepper, you can easily work in more mustard, curry powder, capers, anchovy paste or finely chopped herbs (fresh, please, or don't bother), such as parsley, tarragon, basil, dill or chervil, which lend their flavor to the mayonnaise and speckle it a lovely green.

HOW TO CHOP HERBS: To succeed, you need a large, sharp knife. The best is a standard chef's knife. The worst is a cheap stainless-knife with an upward curving point. You also need a proper cutting surface. Most people use a cutting board, which can be moved into the sink for washing and which keeps you from nicking your counters. Put the herbs on the board in a compact clump. Hold the knife in one hand. Rest the knife point on the board just to the side of the herb clump. Put your other hand on the knife at the point end to anchor it on the board. Now rock the knife up and down, like a paper-cutter blade. Bring it down hard on the herb pile. This action shears the herbs into fragments. As you rock the knife up and down, move it gradually across the pile so that you cover every leaf. After a while, the pile will get spread across the board. Scrape it together with the knife and continue chopping until you have reduced the herbs to a compact mound of green specks. The finer you chop, the more surface area you create and, therefore, the more flavor you release.

HOW TO CHOP GARLIC: Garlic is sold in heads, papery globes slightly larger than walnuts. Each head contains many smaller seedlike cloves. The cloves pull easily away from the head and can be pureed unpeeled in a garlic press. It is just as easy, and produces a less aggressive flavor, to peel and chop garlic with a knife. Put a clove on the cutting board. Rest the flat of the knife on it and pound the knife with your fist to smash the clove underneath. This loosens the skin and makes it easy to remove. Then chop the clove, rocking the knife as you did with the herbs in the paragraph above. Garlic is a powerful seasoning; so add a clove at a time to the mayonnaise until you get the flavor you want. In the south of France, people call a garlic mayonnaise *aioli* (from *ail*, meaning garlic). This dip is the centerpiece for a meal built around raw vegetables that is the origin for most of the raw-vegetable-and-mayonnaise cocktail buffets now so universally seen in this country.

SUGGESTIONS FOR SERVING: Mayonnaise is an ideal accompaniment for cold roast beef, cold shrimps, artichokes, hard-boiled eggs and lobster. But the first thing you might want to try is serving it with raw vegetables, since only a modest amount of knife work will enable you to create a colorful and various table. Any or all of the following vegetables (or others you may find in the market) will be transformed into something special when they are sliced and gracefully arranged around a bowl of flavored mayonnaise. In fact, once you have made the basic mayonnaise, you can divide it into two or three bowls and flavor each one separately so as to multiply the choice of tastes and colors on the table.

CARROTS: Peel with a small knife or vegetable peeler (one of those gadgets with a handle attached to a bladed slot designed to shave the peel off of carrots, potatoes, cucumbers, parsnips, turnips and other vegetables with skins or unappealing outer layers). Slice away the carrot top and the pointy end. Then cut the carrot in half lengthwise. Cut the halves lengthwise into sticks. If the carrot is very long, cut the sticks in half.

SCALLIONS (GREEN ONIONS): Slice away the root end. Peel off the thin outer skin of the white part. Cut off and discard all but two or three inches of the green part.

GREEN, RED AND YELLOW BELL PEPPERS: Slice off the top. Push the stem out of it and discard, keeping the rest. Throw out the seeds and cut the white ribs from the inside and discard. Slice off the bottom. Then slice the pepper lengthwise into strips.

CAULIFLOWER AND BROCCOLI: Snap off the flowerets. Discard what is left.

CUCUMBERS, ZUCCHINI, SUMMER SQUASH: Peel the cucumber only if it has been coated with glistening wax. Scrub the zucchini with a vegetable brush. Slice off both ends of all three. Cut lengthwise into spears.

RADISHES: Wash thoroughly. If the green tops are still attached, trim so as to leave a small handle for dipping. Otherwise, cut a thin slice off the top of the radish. Make sure you cut away any wispy white tails.

Marination

This is the lazy man or woman's route to gracious living. Mix up a seasoned liquid, called a marinade, and leave food to soak in it, to absorb flavors and to mellow. Then eat.

Marinades almost always contain a mildly acidic substance that gently breaks down protein tissue, tenderizing it and "cooking" it without heat. Even when you have full access to a stove, marinated dishes will appeal to you in hot weather, when you can't stand to turn on a burner unnecessarily.

Seviche

Among the most fashionable dishes of our time, this "raw" seafood classic illustrates how the citric acid in lime juice "gentles" the scallops (or fish or shrimp) and makes them seem cooked. But the effect is much more delicate than cooking the same seafood over heat would produce. With seviche, you get the taste of the sea at its purest, with the most minimal investment of your time.

> 1 pound bay scallops, skinned fillets of mackerel or peeled shrimp
> Juice of 8–10 limes (1½ cups)

Salt
Pepper
2 limes cut into wedges

1. If you are using fish, cut it into small cubes. Split shrimp and wash out sand veins (the black line running along the back just under a thin membrane).

2. Place the scallops, mackerel, shrimp or a mixture of the three, weighing a total of 1 pound, into a bowl. Pour in the lime juice. Cover and set in the refrigerator for several hours. Turn several times.

3. When the seafood turns opaque, it should be seasoned with salt and pepper. (Cumin, oregano and Cayenne pepper can be added for personality.)

4. Chill for another hour or so. Then serve, decorated with lime wedges.

YIELD: 4 SERVINGS

Marinated Mushrooms

Simplicity itself, this delicious snack can be stirred together in minutes after breakfast and be ready for cocktails when you get home from the day's work. The mushrooms imbibe the marinade and are subtly softened by it.

1 pound fresh mushrooms
¼ cup wine vinegar
½ cup oil
Salt
Pepper
10 coriander seeds
6 fennel seeds

1. Wipe off the mushrooms. Rinse them lightly in cold water only if they are too dirty just to wipe off. Rinsing removes a certain amount of flavor.

2. Slice large mushrooms in half. Leave the rest whole.

3. Combine all the remaining ingredients in a bowl. Add the mushrooms. Stir to coat with the marinade. Cover and let stand at room temperature several hours. Stir every so often.

YIELD: 4 SERVINGS

Gravlax

This is the famous Swedish method of curing salmon in a dry-spice mixture. Gravlax is more delicate and fresh in taste than the most elite—and costly—smoked salmon.

> 1 boned 2-pound center-cut salmon steak with skin left on
> 4 tablespoons salt
> 2 tablespoons sugar
> 2 tablespoons coarsely ground white pepper
> 1 large bunch fresh dill
> Dill-mustard sauce (see following recipe)

1. Divide the steak into two matching fillets. Pat dry in paper towel.

2. Mix together salt, sugar and white pepper in a small bowl. You can grind the white peppercorns at high speed in a blender.

3. Spread out a double layer of aluminum foil large enough to wrap both salmon fillets. Use a quarter of the dill to make a bed for the salmon.

4. Rub one of the fillets on both sides with about a third of the spice mixture. Lay it skin side down on the dill. Spread an-

other third of the spice mixture on the flesh side of the same fillet. Put another quarter of the dill on top of the spices.

5. Rub the second fillet with the rest of the spices. Lay it on top of the first fillet so that the edges match up but with the thinner long edge of the top piece over the thicker long edge of the bottom piece. Spread a third quarter of the dill over the top piece. Reserve the rest of the dill for the sauce.

6. Wrap the salmon sandwich tightly in the foil. Set on a large plate, place a small cast-iron skillet or other weight on top and refrigerate for 48 hours.

7. Drain the salmon once a day and turn the package each time. Serve on the third day. Slice with a thin, very sharp knife. Gravlax will keep for 3 to 5 days, but must be drained and turned daily.

8. Serve with dill-mustard sauce on the side.

YIELD: 6 TO 8 SERVINGS

Dill-Mustard Sauce for Gravlax

3 tablespoons mild brown-type mustard
1 tablespoon sugar
2 tablespoons white vinegar
½ cup oil
5–6 tablespoons chopped fresh dill (see page 43)
    Salt
    Pepper

1. Mix together mustard, sugar and vinegar in a bowl.

2. Blend oil into this mixture in a slow stream, as for mayonnaise (see page 40).

3. Stir in dill, salt and pepper.

4. Put in a serving bowl and pass with gravlax.

Raw Meat

Steak Tartare

Like many French food names, *tartare* implies an exotic origin for the dish it is applied to. In fact, there is no serious reason to believe that this popular main course of raw ground beef comes to us from the steppes of Tartary in Central Asia. The name is almost certainly the invention of a fanciful chef who found it useful to suggest that the recipe was popular with the wild Tartar horsemen who swept over half the world. Wherever it started, steak tartare is an ideal dish for last-minute preparation, for a late supper after the movies or for a convenient summer meal. It is fun and foolproof to throw together while guests are watching.

> 2 pounds raw ground round or other high-quality steak, such as filet
> 4 egg yolks (see page 41)
> Juice of 1 lemon
> Cayenne pepper
> Salt
> Pepper
> Capers
> 8 anchovy fillets, roughly chopped
> 1 medium onion, chopped (see page 39)

1. In a serving bowl slightly larger than the ground meat, mix all ingredients. Do this in the order that they are listed. Mix in each one gradually so that you can tell how much you want of each, tasting as you go. Be especially careful with the Cayenne pepper, which is very hot. It is also a good idea to ask guests if they want anchovies. To me anchovyphobia is incomprehensible, but it is a widespread problem. You can accommodate this taste prejudice by segregating part of the beef in a separate bowl and

mixing it separately. If you do this, remember that each person gets one egg yolk.

2. Serve with black or rye bread and beer.

YIELD: 4 SERVINGS

Carpaccio

By cleverly slicing and pounding raw beef, you can quite easily convert a plain old steak into one of today's most up-to-the-minute hors d'oeuvres. *Carpaccio* looks beautiful and is actually cheaper than the equivalent amount of fancy prosciutto ham, a delicacy that *carpaccio* wittily imitates.

> **3 pounds boned filet mignon or shell steak, chilled (to make thin slicing easier)**
> **Mayonnaise (see page 40)**

1. Trim the steak to remove all fat. Cut off the tail piece and reserve for stew.

2. Cut the steak into thin slices. You should get at least a dozen slices.

3. Pound the slices, one at a time, with a wooden mallet, until wafer thin. Don't overdo it, however. Overzealous pounding can completely destroy the meat. Quit as soon as you see a hole appear.

4. Chill.

5. Serve with mayonnaise on the side.

YIELD: 6 SERVINGS

Salad

Salad is controversial. Some people serve it at the beginning of the meal. Some bring it on with the main course. Still others, with European practice on their side, serve salad as a separate course between entrée and dessert (some of these people also put cheese on the same plate as the salad, which I think makes a dreadful hodgepodge just to save washing a few plates).

I'm happy with salad at any point in the meal. But you might as well be aware that the European method—a separate course just before dessert—is the classic presentation, and probably the one that makes the most sense to the palate. To serve raw fresh greens and other vegetables dressed with vinaigrette clears the taste buds of the heavier tastes of the main course and makes a clear transition to the sweet tastes of dessert. What it does not do well is accommodate to the wine you may still be drinking. The classic vinaigrette with its vinegar and spices clashes with most wines. Serious wine people sometimes eliminate salad altogether from their meals. It is also quite possible to cleanse the mouth with a drink of water before and after the salad. I find I can ignore this problem quite handily most of the time. It certainly doesn't keep me from eating salad.

Good salad is impossible without good greens. In our markets today there are always several varieties of lettuce available. Unimaginative cooks settle for a head of iceberg lettuce, crisp but bland and watery in flavor. Look instead for greens with more personality—romaine, Bibb, Boston and red lettuce, chicory and tangy arugula (also called rocket) all offer more sophisticated pleasures than iceberg.

Pick the greens that look best. Avoid brown leaves, dry leaves, saggy leaves. A healthy lettuce looks healthy. You should be able to find at least two acceptable varieties of lettuce at any time of year. And it is almost always more interesting to mix different greens in the same salad. A salad is, after all, a mixture. That's why we call the verbal gibberish of the insane "word salad."

I like to throw all sorts of things besides lettuce into salads—

chopped green peppers, broccoli flowerets, croutons, anchovy fillets, sliced radishes. But there are really only two things that are essential to a successful salad: good, clean lettuce and a good dressing.

Having purchased excellent lettuce, you must wash it carefully to remove the grit it picked up while pushing through the soil. Lettuce may look clean, but it is sheerest folly to serve it unwashed. Sandy salad is an abomination and an unnecessary embarrassment.

Fill the sink with cold water. Pull the leaves off the lettuce head, discarding any that are old or wilted or stained with brown. Tear large leaves into smaller pieces (since it is bad manners to cut salad with a knife, you do everyone a favor by tearing lettuce down to size, making the pieces small enough so that they only have to be cut once with the side of a fork to be conveniently edible). Place all the lettuce in the sink. Swirl it around. You will probably be rewarded with the sight of black specks floating to the bottom of the sink. Then scoop out the leaves and dry them. No, not one by one. You can spread them out on a length of paper toweling and then roll it up to remove the moisture. Or you can spin the lettuce in one of the new plastic lettuce driers, which are inexpensive, durable, effective and fun to use.

The point of drying lettuce is to improve its ability to sop up dressing. Wet lettuce tends to glide through an oil-and-vinegar dressing and come out clean. This is just the opposite of what you will be hoping for when you toss the lettuce together with your classic vinaigrette (see recipe below).

This is the only dressing I'm giving a recipe for. It's not that I want to discourage you from serving blue-cheese dressing, Russian dressing or celery-seed dressing. Well, maybe I do. A basic vinaigrette enhances the salad. Heavier, gloppier dressings and dressings with aggressive spices or sugar swamp the delicate tastes of interesting greens. Blue cheese and the other dressings you find on salad bars in second-rate restaurants are best suited to go with insipid iceberg lettuce. Vinaigrette goes just far enough in declaring its own virtues, but not too far.

Vinaigrette Dressing

If you'd rather call this an oil-and-vinegar dressing, go right ahead. Just please don't Americanize the name into *vinegarette*. There's nothing that sets the teeth on edge like pseudo-French.

¾ cup oil
¼ cup wine vinegar
   Salt
   Pepper
1 clove garlic, minced (see page 43)
1 tablespoon imported white-wine mustard (optional)

1. In a bowl or a glass measuring cup, combine all ingredients. Stir together with a fork. Let stand during the meal so that flavors blend together.

It makes a great deal of difference which oil and which vinegar you put in this dressing. Obviously. But the range of choice in both oils and vinegars is so great that it would be fruitless to attempt a survey of even the leading varieties here. In general, if you like the taste of olive oil, use olive oil. If you don't, don't. Finding an olive oil you do like is as complex and as much fun as picking a wine you like.

So-called salad oils (extracted from peanuts, corn or other vegetable seeds and nuts) are relatively neutral in taste. This is, however, not true of walnut oil, an expensive and assertive but delicious oil that can be used alone or mixed in with another, blander oil.

Vinegars range from the pure acetic sold as white vinegar in most supermarkets to those cultured from red or white wine or cider. Some vinegars come flavored with herbs, especially tarragon and sage. Italian balsamic vinegars are particularly intense and give the dressing a thick, velvety consistency. In general, you should try to take into account the individual characters of your oil and your vinegar, balancing their tastes by altering the basic proportions of one part vinegar to three parts oil so that you achieve a dressing you like. In our family, we like the acidity that extra vinegar brings. You may prefer more oil to mask the vinegar. Experience will show the way.

Some refined souls dispense with vinegar altogether. They use only lemon juice, because it is less fiercely acid than vinegar. I think this is prissy if it is raised to the level of obsession. But a lemon vinaigrette is a fine thing to try when lemons are cheap and you are using a delicate lettuce such as Bibb.

Mustard not only imparts its own flavor to the dressing but also helps it stay together as a uniform, "creamy" sauce.

People add all kinds of other ingredients to vinaigrettes—capers, Cayenne pepper, chives, chopped parsley—but none of this is essential. I think it interferes with the purity and point of a vinaigrette in the first place.

The quantity produced by this recipe is just enough for a large salad that will serve a dinner for eight. You can easily make a smaller amount by dividing the ingredients proportionally. But vinaigrette will keep perfectly well, even unrefrigerated, for a day or so.

Basic Green Salad

1 head romaine, washed and dried (see page 52)
1 head Bibb, washed and dried
½ recipe vinaigrette dressing (see previous recipe)

1. Refrigerate the lettuce in a plastic bag until ready to serve.
2. Tear leaves and put in a serving bowl. Just before serving, stir the vinaigrette to make sure it is evenly blended and pour it over the lettuce.
3. Toss with two wooden spoons or a wooden spoon and fork. Some exhibitionists actually toss the lettuce into the air. It is quite enough to stir the lettuce pieces thoroughly in the dressing so that they are completely coated. This should be done at the last minute. A salad tossed ahead of time will turn sodden.

4. The quantity of lettuce given here is highly approximate. One head of romaine will probably serve six. After you've torn the lettuce into servable pieces, you ought to have a much better idea of how much to serve. As you put the lettuce pieces in the serving bowl, try to imagine how much you will want to eat yourself and multiply by the number of people you'll be serving. Stop when you've put enough in the bowl and refrigerate the rest for future use. Washed dry lettuce should keep in the refrigerator for a day or so.

This basic salad can be varied almost infinitely, substituting other greens, adding sliced tomatoes, cucumbers and other ingredients, those listed above in the general discussion of salad and a myriad of others that you will come up with yourself.

YIELD: 8 SERVINGS

Tomato Salad

This is the simplest of all salads, but also the most difficult. The restaurant critic of the Parisian newspaper *Le Monde* once rated several highly regarded French restaurants solely on the basis of their tomato salads. How these establishments treated such a simple dish was a test of their fundamental seriousness. Were the tomatoes perfectly fresh and tart from the vine? Had they been sliced uniformly thin just before they were served? Were the slices attractively arranged? Was the vinaigrette well made? These same questions face any of us when we set out to serve a tomato salad. In this country, there is the added problem of avoiding those hybrid toughies engineered to ripen in a gas-filled truck and with flesh thick enough and strong enough to endure the trip without blemish. These tomatoes are not worth buying. They have virtually no taste. They are crunchy instead of voluptuously soft. A naturally ripe, genetically traditional tomato is a test for a sharp knife. In fact, ripe tomatoes are so difficult to slice without squashing that gourmet shops sell special serrated tomato knives that do the job ideally well.

8 medium tomatoes
16 fresh basil leaves (optional)
½ recipe vinaigrette dressing (see page 53)

1. With a very sharp knife, cut out the green circle where the tomato stem was. Some tomatoes also have a white, tough area just below this green circle. Remove it also with the point of the knife.

2. Hold the tomato against a cutting board with one hand. It should be placed so that the hole left from removing the stem section is pointing to the side facing the knife and will be at the center of the first slice. Slice the tomato as thinly as you can. When you have worked your way halfway through, turn it around and continue slicing from what was originally the bottom of the tomato (the place opposite the stem). This switch gives you a larger place to grip. Even so, it may be impossible to cut quite such thin slices at the very end, when you are holding only a thin remnant of the tomato. At this point, lay it flat on the board. Steady it gently with one hand and cut through the remainder of the tomato with the knife held sideways.

3. As you finish slicing each tomato, arrange its slices on an individual salad plate.

4. If you can find fresh basil leaves, chop them roughly, rocking the knife (see page 43), and sprinkle over the tomato slices. Then stir the vinaigrette until well blended and pour over the tomatoes on each plate.

5. This salad should only be served when tomatoes that are not mass-produced are available. In most places, that means high summer. As a variation, you can use half the quantity of tomatoes and insert a thin slice of mozzarella cheese between each tomato slice. Basil leaves are traditional with this dish.

YIELD: 8 SERVINGS

Cucumbers in Dilled Yogurt

In the dead of sultry summer, what could be better than starting a meal with the cool crunch of fresh cucumber made cooler still with dill-flavored yogurt? The somewhat elaborate draining of the cucumber is worth it, in spades, because you can store the leftovers in the refrigerator or prepare the dish in advance without having water leach out of the cucumber into the yogurt. Also, you get rid of the seeds, which are no help to anyone except cucumber gardeners, who can save them if they want.

> 2 medium cucumbers
> Salt (optional)
> 2 cups plain yogurt
> 1 tablespoon snipped fresh dill *or* 2 teaspoons dried dill

1. Almost all supermarket cucumbers are coated with a protective, beautifying wax. Therefore, they must be peeled with a vegetable peeler (see page 44). Untreated cucumbers should be left unpeeled. No matter which kind you have, slice off both ends and discard. Then slice into thin rounds.

(A slightly more arduous, but perhaps more elegant, method eliminates the seeds and excess water. Cut the cucumbers into quarters lengthwise. Slice out the seeds and discard. Then salt the quartered cucumbers liberally and leave them to drain for several hours in a colander, a metal bowl with large perforations meant for draining steamed vegetables and pasta. Rinse away excess salt. Then cut into chunks and proceed as with the sliced cucumber rounds.)

2. Drain any excess water out of the yogurt. Stir the dill into it. Then add the cucumber. Stir well and serve.

YIELD: 6–8 SERVINGS

Cole Slaw

If you have never eaten homemade cole slaw, you may be turning up your deprived nose at the idea of spending time on this excellent dish just because you have only tasted it at fast-food restaurants. But we are not talking about tired, watery slaw popped out next to thin burgers in wee paper cuplets. We are talking about a fresh, delicious, cheap and elegant salad. Cut the cabbage in the thinnest slices you can for the best result. Serve anytime, especially when the lettuce in your market is looking poorly. Cabbage is a friend in need.

1 **large head cabbage**
1 **medium onion, chopped (see page 39)**
¾ **cup mayonnaise (see page 40)**
   Salt
   Pepper

1. Remove blemished or dry outer leaves of cabbage and discard. Cut out the hard core and discard. Then slice the cabbage into fine shreds with a big, sharp knife.
2. Combine the cabbage shreds, chopped onion and mayonnaise in a serving bowl. Stir well. Taste and season if necessary with salt and pepper.

YIELD: 8 SERVINGS

VARIATIONS: Feel free to add shredded carrot; just cut it into very fine strips (see page 44) or put it through the julienne blade on a processor. (One large carrot will probably suffice.) Some people like to add a tablespoon of caraway seeds.

Fruit

To soak fruit in a sweetened liquid, especially one spiked with liqueur, is to practice maceration. I would keep this bit of technical knowledge to myself. But the process itself is something you will find gains you credit with the general public. The liquid draws out some of the juices from the fruit, creating a sort of spontaneously generated fruit sauce. Meanwhile, the flavors of the macerating liquid penetrate the fruit.

Strawberries in Orange Sauce

Simple as this is, it will nicely complete the most elegant meal. But it is not worth doing except at the height of the strawberry season, when the fruit is tip-top and you have already begun to be jaded by eating strawberries as is.

>   1 pint box strawberries
>   1 cup orange juice
>   1 tablespoon sugar
>   1 tablespoon Cointreau, or other orange-flavored liqueur (optional)

1. With a small knife, cut away the green tops of the strawberries as well as the white part underneath them.

2. Slice the strawberries in half. Cut very large ones in quarters.

3. In a shallow bowl, stir the orange juice together with the sugar and the Cointreau until the sugar dissolves. Then add the sliced strawberries. Stir gently.

4. Refrigerate for several hours, stirring from time to time.

YIELD: 4 SERVINGS

Pineapple with Kirsch

Kirsch (sometimes called kirschwasser) is a distilled drink made from cherries. By itself, it is as powerfully alcoholic as whiskey. But as a flavoring, it brings out the pineapple's own taste, which, in turn, softens the bite of the kirsch. Pineapple with kirsch is a standard dessert in French restaurants. But you can improve on French practice by serving fresh, instead of canned, fruit. By world standards, pineapples in this country are cheap. The trick is to buy a ripe one. Avoid obviously damaged pineapples with wet spots indicating overripeness. I have had very good luck with the slightly more expensive Hawaiian pineapples.

> 1 fresh pineapple
> 1 cup kirsch, approximately

1. Cut the top off the pineapple. Then slice it into quarters, lengthwise. This will expose a woody core running down the middle of each quarter. Cut away these core pieces and discard. Next, cut away the skin of the pineapple: Insert the point of the knife between the skin and the flesh. Then slice the skin away from the flesh on each side of each quarter.

2. Slice the peeled pineapple into wedges.

3. Put the wedges in a serving bowl. Pour the kirsch over them. Refrigerate for several hours, stirring occasionally to make sure the kirsch is well distributed over the pineapple.

YIELD: 4 SERVINGS

Drinks

Alfred Knopf, the publisher, was also a serious wine drinker, with a cellar full of important old bottles. But at lunch in the summer, he liked to take iced coffee with his meal. When he moved his company to its current location on the east side of Manhattan, he thought he would try out the French restaurant across the street. The owner, a man named Fayet, refused to serve Knopf his iced coffee. From then on, no one from Knopf's firm ate at Fayet's. That was a lot of expense-account lunching that went elsewhere. Fayet is no longer in business in New York.

In drinking, there are no rules. Somewhere in the world you will find an entire culture doing exactly what comes naturally to you—Swedes swilling hard liquor right through the meal, or Italians pouring white wine to go with rare lamb because the wine comes from the next hill and is cold when the weather is hot.

But you might as well know what the rules, in so-called polite society, are supposed to be. The wine writer Alexis Bespaloff put it all in a nutshell when he recorded a message for his telephone answering machine: "If it's an emergency, remember: red with meat, white with fish."

The joke was funny for two reasons. Any friend of Bespaloff's ought to have known already about the basic red-white split in matching food and wine. What was really funny was that Bespaloff was thumbing his nose at those very specific "marriages" of food and wine that the slick magazines and the wine experts like to natter on about.

Now it is probably true that a heavy, earthy red wine like Châteauneuf-du-Pape from the south of France near Avignon will stand up against game better than a delicate red from farther north. But you mustn't become a slave of this sort of theory. If all you've got to serve with your bear haunch is Beaujolais, don't blush.

The truth is that the best guide to matching wine and food is your experience. Trying to build meals around textbook-perfect marriages between specific dishes and specific labels is a ridiculous idea. Half the time you won't even be able to find the particular wine that's been recommended anyway.

Some advice will hold true for all levels of experience and budget. Chill all white wine. Let white wines you think are more complex in flavor come back a little toward room temperature before serving.

Lightly chill some light, uncomplicated red wines, particularly Beaujolais. But don't let anyone tell you that opening a red wine a bit ahead of time will improve its flavor. This theory has been disproved over and over. In addition, a wine opened and then held overnight will lose finesse and sometimes degrade irretrievably through oxidation.

If you want to learn more about wines, look at Bespaloff's inexpensive and authoritative *Signet Book of Wines*. Or take a class. Or open several wines at the same time with friends and taste them against each other. This is the classic and only method of developing your wine palate.

Hard Stuff

In the early part of this century, cocktails were all the rage. Recipes for these mixed drinks are recorded in easily available bartender's guides that will allow anybody with a will to shake together Manhattans and Fluffy Ruffles and Pink Ladies. Most of this kind of thing is wildly out of date, especially in private homes, where nobody today is expected to do more than put ice in a glass and throw whiskey or gin after it. In any case, this is not a bartender's guide, and I'm basically in favor of suppressing the consumption of distilled spirits (hard liquor) before meals, because they numb the perception of taste. However, you might as well be prepared to make a few classic drinks.

Martini

The preeminent sophisticated cocktail, the martini has survived into the age of white wine. It can be made easily and well in the home. But watch out. The martini can be lethal.

> 1½ ounces 90-proof gin
> Dry (white) vermouth
> Lemon peel or cocktail olive

Martini is the name of an Italian vermouth manufacturer. Vermouth is a sort of flavored wine that comes sweet (red) or dry (white). Most people who drink lots of martinis don't pay any attention to these facts. They have discovered that a very cold mixture of gin with a very tiny admixture of white vermouth of any brand will produce a lethal cocktail.

Many martini fanciers have turned this drink into a kind of religion. They rhapsodize about the catalytic effect that a drop or two of vermouth has on a glass of gin. They don't shake these cocktails. They stir them with an ice cube or two, then discard the ice cube. Most people will gladly accept a martini on the rocks.

The dry martini is definitely a departure from the original drink, which included much higher proportions of vermouth. Almost no one drinks them that way anymore. Most people do, however, like a flavoring element superadded to the basic mix. Real traditionalists like small pitted green olives. More modern folk opt for "a twist." Ideally, this means a shaving of the yellow outer portion of the lemon's peel, cut away with a vegetable peeler and rubbed around the edge of the glass, snapped or cracked to release lemon oil into the drink and then dropped into the glass. If you use cocktail onions instead, you have made a Gibson. A martini with nothing added, not even vermouth, is called a naked martini.

All martinis taste good but do not promote fine distinctions in taste or other areas of intellectual discrimination.

YIELD: 1 COCKTAIL

Grog

Cures whatever ails you. Keeps the cold out. Grog is hot-flavored rum, a wonderful warm-up after skiing or almost anytime in the winter.

> 2 tablespoons rum
> 1 teaspoon sugar
> ½ stick cinnamon
> ¼ cup boiling water

1. Combine rum and sugar in a mug or tumbler. Add cinnamon.
2. Pour water over rum and sugar. Stir and serve immediately.

YIELD: 1 GROG

Bloody Mary

This is the classic American eye-opener. *The* drink to serve at brunch. It was named after a Polynesian character in the Rodgers and Hammerstein musical comedy *South Pacific*. By legend, it was invented in the old bar of the St. Regis Hotel in New York City. Almost everything in this recipe is optional except the tomato juice. There should also be some kind of spicing. Without booze, it's a Virgin Mary.

> 1½ cups of vodka
> 4 cups tomato juice
> Salt
> Pepper
> Cayenne pepper
> Worcestershire sauce

1. Combine the vodka and tomato juice in a pitcher and stir.

2. Gradually mix in the spices. Taste as you go, but leave some for the others. It should be pungent but bearable. The flavors will intensify if you hold the mixture for several hours. Cayenne pepper is a very potent ingredient.

3. Chill.

YIELD: 8 SERVINGS

3

DESSERTS, SNACKS, TREATS

IN ANY NORMAL MEAL, THE SWEETS COME LAST. BUT FOR MANY people who cook, they come first. Because desserts tend to take more time and technique, and because, once finished, they keep well, practiced cooks tackle them first on most menus. Cakes and pies, and candy, cookies and fudge, which require far more precision to make than almost any main course, are also the first dishes that most of us learn to make. They can be served all by themselves to friends who drop over. They satisfy our sweet tooth. And they let us show off our abilities in the kitchen without forcing us to pull out all the stops and rustle up a complete meal.

Offer brownies and you are a host from whom no one expects more. Apple pie is a meal in itself. Indeed, in colonial days, settlers really did make whole suppers out of them all through the winter, since a whole harvest of apples could be dried and kept without refrigeration.

It is every child's fantasy to eat dessert first. And I think that this dream persists in all of us after we have grown too big to admit it. But anyone who learns to make some of the standard desserts and snacks that everyone loves can indulge this suppressed desire from time to time, smugly self-sufficient and happy in the knowledge that baked goods bought in stores are marked up higher over the cost of their raw materials than any other commercially prepared foods.

Putting desserts first, before all the other cooked dishes in this book, I am also giving in to a sentimental preference of my own. If you prefer to wait till later and move on to first things first, skip ahead to the next chapter. Me, I'm feeling like a brownie.

Brownies

These chocolate-laden squares are the most popular of all American snacks. Everyone in this culture who cooks bakes brownies, and often brownies are the first thing they have cooked. Brownies are quick, require a minimum of technique and usually turn out delicious even for rank beginners. Yet, like most things everyone knows about and cares about, brownies are controversial. There is no single authentic recipe or standard. Some people add chopped walnuts, some like raisins, others ice their brownies. Purists indulge in none of these frills, but they still disagree about the fundamental issue in brownie making: Are brownies a form of cake verging toward fudge or a form of fudge verging toward cake? I am a fudgeite but not fanatic about it. So here are two recipes. The first is fudgy; the second, cakey. Both make small batches. You can easily double these recipes, but then you should use a larger rectangular baking pan with a surface area of roughly 110 square inches (for instance, a 9 × 12-inch pan) instead of the approximately 50 square inches of the 7 × 7-inch pan prescribed below.

Finally, remember that brownies are no better than the chocolate or cocoa you start with. If you can, buy best quality imported chocolate and cocoa.

Brownies I

1 cup sugar
¼ pound (1 stick) butter at room temperature
1 ounce unsweetened chocolate
2 eggs, lightly beaten
7 tablespoons cocoa
⅛ teaspoon salt

½ cup all-purpose flour
1 cup roughly chopped walnuts (optional)
1 teaspoon vanilla

1. Preheat oven to 350 degrees.

2. Grease and lightly flour a baking pan, 7 × 7 inches or 8 × 8 inches. Holding a small piece of butter with a bit of paper towel, smear the bottom and sides of the pan. Then pour in ¼ cup of flour, shake pan to distribute evenly on bottom and sides, and dump out any loose flour. Set aside.

3. Beat the sugar and butter together in an electric mixer until smooth.

4. Melt chocolate in a small pan immersed in boiling water or in a double boiler. Scrape into sugar-butter mixture. Add eggs and beat until smooth.

5. Fold in cocoa, salt and flour, gradually. When the mixture is smooth and of uniform color, beat in nuts and vanilla.

6. Scrape the batter into the prepared baking pan with a rubber spatula. Spread so that it fills the pan evenly.

7. Bake for 25 minutes or until a skewer inserted into the center comes out clean. Do not overbake. Good brownies should be moist.

8. Cool on a wire rack. Brownies must reach room temperature to set properly. Then cut them into rectangles of whatever size you like.

YIELD: ABOUT 1 DOZEN BROWNIES

Brownies II

¼ pound (1 stick) butter
2 ounces unsweetened chocolate
2 eggs
1 cup sugar
½ teaspoon vanilla
¼ cup all-purpose flour
¼ cup roughly chopped walnuts (optional)

1. Preheat oven to 350 degrees.

2. Grease and lightly flour a 7 × 7- or 8 × 8-inch baking pan (see page 70). Set aside.

3. Cut up butter into small pieces. Break up chocolate. Put butter and chocolate into a small pan or the top of a double boiler and melt over boiling water. Set aside to cool.

4. With a balloon whisk or an electric mixer, beat eggs and sugar until smooth and colored light yellow.

5. Beat in vanilla. Then beat in chocolate-butter mixture. Then fold in flour. When the mixture is smooth and of uniform color, mix in nuts.

6. Scrape batter into prepared baking pan with a rubber spatula. Distribute evenly in the pan and bake for 25 minutes or until a skewer inserted into the center comes out clean. Do not overbake. Brownies should be moist.

7. Cool on a wire rack. Brownies will not set properly until they reach room temperature. Then cut them into rectangles of the size you want.

YIELD: ABOUT 1 DOZEN BROWNIES

Pies

Americans love eating pies, but they hate making them. The crust is the universal stumbling block. Pie fillings are generally easy as pie, so to speak. But making a crust is a precise business. The idea is to blend cold butter into flour, but not to blend it so completely that you produce a lead crust instead of a flaky one.

Once you've mixed up the dough, however, it can be easily frozen and kept until the time when you want to roll it out. So it makes sense to prepare pie-crust dough in fairly large quantity. That's why the crust recipe below is designed to produce enough dough for two double-crusted pies or four single-crusted ones.

Pie Crust
(With thanks to Wilma Priebe)

3 cups flour

1 teaspoon salt

1 cup (8 ounces) butter, lard or margarine (flakiest results are with lard or margarine; best taste with
butter; least interesting taste with margarine. You
can strike a nice balance by combining 2 ounces of
lard with 6 ounces of butter.)

1 tablespoon vinegar

5 tablespoons cold water

1 egg

1. In a large bowl, combine flour, salt, and butter, lard or
margarine, which should be refrigerator cold. Slice whichever form
of shortening you use into pats or small chunks. (In pastry recipes,
short means containing fat or shortening of some kind—butter, lard,
margarine, vegetable shortening. A short pastry has a lot of shortening, as does that Scottish confection shortbread.)

Don't hesitate at this point. Let the phone ring. The idea is to
"cut" the fat into the flour without letting it melt and to spread
it uniformly through the eventual dough. You want to end up with
a substance that looks like raw oatmeal: flour flecked with little
nuggets of butter, lard or margarine. A crust made from such a
dough is flaky, because when the crust is baked the bits of fat have
the effect of producing distinct layers of pastry—flakes. The same
process is exploited systematically to produce the hundreds of layers in a strudel dough: The butter, in effect, fries each layer separately inside the dough while it bakes. A successful pie crust is
an informal example of this basic idea. You want to infiltrate
moistened flour with little landmines of fat that will, in turn, cook
the innumerable minipastries that comprise a crust—and keep them
from sticking to each other. Instead, they flake when you attack
them with a fork.

The worst thing to do to a crust dough is touch it with your hot little hands. Cold steel is the best tool for cutting in fat. Any housewares store carries pastry blenders specially made for this job. They consist of a handle attached to several semicircular wires. You just hold on and punch away at the dough until the butter is cut in. If you don't have a pastry blender, use two dinner forks.

2. In another bowl, whisk together the vinegar, water and egg until well mixed. Then blend thoroughly into the dough with a wooden spoon, a little at a time. As you do this, the dough should gather itself into a solid, fairly dry mass. Don't worry if a few crumbs won't adhere.

3. Divide dough into four equal pieces. Your eye should be able to estimate this division accurately enough. For perfection, use a scale.

Even if you intend to use the dough the same day you've made it, refrigerate in a plastic bag for an hour. Otherwise, bag and freeze. Put a label on the bag.

4. Rolling the crust: If the dough has been frozen, defrost in the refrigerator. Leave several hours for this. When you are ready to roll out the crust, preheat oven to 450 degrees. Take one of the pieces of dough from the refrigerator and set it on the center of a sheet of lightly floured wax paper about a foot long. Lay another sheet of floured wax paper the same size on top of the dough. The wax paper makes it easy to move the rolled out dough from counter to pie pan. Dough tends to stick to the counter, otherwise, and you would have to keep sprinkling flour on the counter and on the rolling pin to prevent sticking. Even then, you would have the devil's own time easing the thin, delicate sheet of dough off the counter. A couple of metal spatulas help a lot, but why bother when cheap wax paper makes all this easy.

Flatten the dough by pressing on it with a rolling pin. Then start rolling from the center of the dough to the outsides, squeezing it into a thin circle of dough. Turn the dough as you roll, so that you are rolling uniformly. The idea is to end up with a roughly circular piece of dough about ⅛-inch thick and big enough to fill a 9-inch pie pan.

If you're not sure you've rolled the dough into a large enough circle, take a pie pan, invert it and set it over the dough. The dough should be a bit larger than the circle described by the edge of the inverted pan, to account for the angle of the pan's sides.

Carefully strip away the top piece of wax paper. Now take hold of the bottom sheet of wax paper. The dough will stick to it, so you can use the paper as a kind of handle to move the dough to the (ungreased) pie pan. Invert and set the dough into the pan. Center it. Press it into the pan, all the while touching only the wax paper. Now carefully strip away the "bottom" sheet of wax paper, which is now on top of the dough.

5. Prick holes all over the bottom of the crust with a fork. This helps the crust bake crisply without getting damp. With your sharpest small knife, trim off any excess dough hanging over the edge of the pie pan. Use these pieces to patch any holes in the crust or places where the dough doesn't quite reach the edge of the pan. Moisten these patches before pressing them in place. Then crimp the edge of the crust by pressing the tines of a fork against it all the way around the top edge of the pie pan.

Cherry Pie

Classic American cherry pies are made from tart pie cherries that are not generally sold as whole fruit in big-city markets. The cherry pie we all know, even when homemade, is almost always made from canned pie cherries preserved in a sugar syrup that itself becomes an ingredient in the recipe. The classic recipe also includes a noticeable amount of cornstarch. If you like classic American cherry pies, as I do, almost the only practical and sensible way to make one is to buy 2 cans of ready-made canned pie filling, pour them into a pie crust, put on the top crust and bake at 400 degrees for 30 minutes. The crust will be much better than you normally get in bakeries and restaurants. And there is not much point in looking down your nose at canned filling, since that is the classic filling for this pie.

Apple Pie

This recipe won the apple-pie contest at a county fair in Iowa. The heavy cream is what sets it apart from standard apple pies. During baking, the cream and juice from the apples mix to form an especially smooth, luxurious sauce bathing the apples.

3½ cups peeled, cored and sliced tart cooking apples
1 cup sugar
2 tablespoons flour
1 teaspoon vanilla extract
⅔ cup heavy cream
1 or 2 pie crusts (see previous recipe)

1. If you aren't sure which apples in your market are for cooking, ask the vegetable man or almost any older customer. As long as you avoid sweet eating apples such as Delicious, you will be all right. To peel: Use a small paring knife. Cut out the area around the stem. Then, hold the apple in one hand and rotate it as you cut away the peel, working the knife around the apple, cutting away a thin longitudinal strip until the fruit is peeled. This gets easier after you've done a few.

Cut the peeled apples in quarters, from stem to stern. The core is a papery section at the center of the fruit that harbors the seeds. Cut away core and seeds and discard. Now slice the cored apples into ⅛-inch lengthwise slices.

2. Preheat oven to 450 degrees.

3. Mix together the apple slices, sugar, flour, vanilla and cream in a bowl.

4. Roll out the dough for 1 crust and put in a 9-inch pie pan (see page 73). Spread filling evenly in the pie crust.

5. If you want a double-crusted pie, roll out a second piece of dough. Moisten the edge of the bottom crust. Set the second crust on top of the pie and press around the edges. With a sharp knife, trim and then slash through the top crust in several places or cut a small hole at the center to let steam escape, so that the top crust bakes crisply.

6. Bake 10 minutes. Then reduce oven temperature to 350 degrees and bake another 30 to 40 minutes, until crust is nicely browned and apples are tender when poked with a fork (poke right through the top crust if you are using one).

Cool on a rack. There are small wire platforms sold for this purpose: to raise pastry off the counter so that it cools uniformly and quickly.

Pecan Pie

This Southern favorite is the only reason most people have a bottle of corn syrup in their kitchen. The syrup keeps almost forever, but it is much easier to open the second time if you haven't twisted the cap tight. Just set it down securely on the bottle—that way it won't stick tight. This will also work for bottles of honey, molasses, sorghum molasses—any of the liquid natural surrogates for white sugar. Another secret is that this recipe works quite well with walnuts, which are cousins of the pecan. Also, unless you live in a pecan-growing area, it is probably cheaper to buy shelled pecans than to pay premium prices for pecans in the shell, which usually taste no better and have to be cracked.

> 3 eggs, lightly beaten
> ½ cup sugar
> 1 cup dark corn syrup
> 1 teaspoon vanilla extract
> ¼ teaspoon salt
> 1½ cups pecans
> 1 stick (½ cup or 8 tablespoons) unsalted butter, cut into pats and melted over low heat
> 1 pie crust in a 9-inch pie pan (see page 72)

1. Preheat oven to 425 degrees.
2. In a large bowl, combine the eggs, sugar, corn syrup, va-

nilla extract, salt, pecans and butter together thoroughly and pour into the pie crust.

3. Bake in the middle level of the oven for 15 minutes. Reduce heat to 350 degrees. Then bake 20 minutes more or until the pie, which is really a custard, sets. Stick a knife point into the filling and look to see that the filling is solid and no longer runny.

Cakes

Cheesecake

Since it has a crust made from graham crackers, perhaps this New York specialty is not really a cake at all, but a pie. Call it what you like, but don't follow the corrupt path of Manhattan delis that gussy up cheesecake with cherry topping, chocolate, nuts and anything else they can think of. It is best by itself, thick with eggs, tangy from sour cream, pure white and pure pleasure.

The crust doesn't have to be rolled, and it is therefore foolproof. The trick here is slow cooking and overnight refrigeration, which lets the cake firm up and develop flavor.

12–14 whole graham crackers
  1 cup sugar
  8 tablespoons (1 stick) butter, melted
1½ pounds cream cheese, left at room temperature to soften
  4 eggs
  1 teaspoon vanilla
  1 cup sour cream

1. Preheat oven to 325 degrees.
2. Pulverize the graham crackers in a processor fitted with the

metal blade, or crumble them between sheets of wax paper, a few at a time, with a rolling pin.

3. In a bowl, combine the cracker crumbs, ¼ cup sugar and the melted butter. Stir until well combined. Then press the crumb mixture evenly over the bottom and an inch up the sides of a 9-inch springform pan (these are inexpensive and useful cake pans sold almost everywhere, including supermarkets; a spring latch allows the circular wall of the pan to be removed after baking so that delicate cakes can be unmolded without harm).

4. With an electric mixer, beat the cream cheese until it fills with air and palpably lightens. Then beat in the remaining ¾ cup sugar until smooth. Beat in the eggs and vanilla, and continue beating for 5 minutes at high speed.

5. Fold in sour cream. This is a gentle form of mixing. It will keep the beaten eggs from deflating. Just put all the sour cream into the bowl with the batter. Then cut into the center of the batter with the side of a rubber spatula. Fold up the batter from below on top of the sour cream. Continue in this way, rotating the bowl and cutting into the mixture, until the sour cream is completely blended in.

6. Pour batter into crust. Smooth the top with a rubber spatula and bake in the middle level of the oven for an hour or until a toothpick inserted in the filling comes out almost clean.

7. Let cool to room temperature in its pan. Chill in the refrigerator for 12 hours, covered with a plate. Remove spring-latched sides and place the cake, still on its metal circle, on a serving platter and serve at room temperature.

Chocolate Cake

This is a moist, rich chocolate cake with two layers and a chocolate icing. Although loosely based on a recipe from the three-star French restaurant run by Georges Blanc in the village of Vonnas near Lyons, it is simpler than many ordinary American chocolate cakes of no distinction whatever.

Instead of adding baking soda to the batter to lighten it, M. Blanc uses whole eggs, beaten unseparated—following, for the most part, the classic procedures for making the preeminent, classic French cake, the *génoise*. His recipe (which I have doubled so as to turn it into a layer cake) actually eliminates some of the problems of the normal *génoise*, but not the main one. By tradition, it is necessary to hand whisk a *génoise* batter for 10 minutes in order to force air into the heavy egg batter. When I was at *The New York Times*, readers failed to accomplish this in droves, and they wrote angry letters. The answer is to have the eggs at room temperature and to use an electric mixer—the more powerful, the better.

This is a wonderful cake, light and dense simultaneously, moist, richly chocolate, attractive.

> 9 ounces sweet baking chocolate (sold in your super-market's baking ingredients section in packages of 1-ounce cubes or in bars marked off in fractions of an ounce)
> 14 tablespoons (1¾ sticks) unsalted butter
> ¾ cup (3½ ounces) all-purpose flour (scooped directly out of the bag with a ¼-cup measuring cup. Level off each time with a knife.)
> 1½ cups sugar
> 8 eggs, beaten until smoothly blended
> Apricot preserves
> 1 recipe chocolate icing (see page 81)
> Unsweetened cocoa powder

1. Preheat oven to 350 degrees. Set a cookie sheet on the middle rack in the oven. This eliminates hot spots from the wires in the rack.

2. Pour an inch or so of water into a shallow pan and bring to a boil. Meanwhile, grease the bottom and inner walls of two 9-inch round cake pans and line the bottoms with greased wax paper

circles. Use the pans as templates for cutting the wax paper circles: Set a pan on the paper and, while holding it down with one hand, score the paper with a knife point, using the bottom edge of the pan as a guide. After you've placed the greased circles in the pans, dump a very small amount of flour in each and shake to coat bottoms and sides with a thin dust of flour. Tilt the pans and shake out any excess flour.

3. Put the chocolate, broken into pieces, and the butter, cut into pats, in the top of a double boiler. Bring water in the bottom of the double boiler to a boil and place chocolate-butter mixture over it. Let the chocolate and butter melt while stirring with a wooden spoon. As soon as the mixture is melted, lift the top pan out of the bottom pan and set aside. The mixture will stay melted long enough for you to prepare the rest of the cake batter. But don't hesitate at this point. Go right to the next step.

4. In a bowl, mix together the flour, sugar and eggs.

5. Pour the chocolate-butter mixture into the egg mixture. Use a rubber spatula to get all the chocolate out of the saucepan. Then beat the batter at high speed in an electric mixer for several minutes, until it is smooth and the spatula leaves a trace as you move it across the surface. This "ribbon" should last for a bit, not fade immediately. This is crucial to the success of the recipe. The batter should end up so stiff it is almost impossible to pour.

6. Fill each cake pan with half the batter. Bake for 30 minutes. A toothpick or trussing needle inserted into the cake should come out clean.

7. While the cake is still hot from the oven, run a knife or a thin, narrow icing spatula around the sides of each layer to make sure it is not sticking to the mold. Invert the pans on pastry racks or plates. To do this, start with the cake pan sitting on a counter, set the rack or plate on top, then, using a potholder if necessary, pick up the entire package, with one hand on top and the other on the bottom, and invert. The layers should pop out easily. Then carefully peel off the wax paper. Let the layers cool.

8. Set one layer on a serving plate. Spread the surface with apricot preserves. Set the other layer on top of the first, with the

bottom side up (this gives you a model flat surface as the top of your cake). Then spread the top and sides of the cake with the icing. You can do this with an icing spatula or a dinner knife, covering the top first and then coating the sides. Remove any icing spills from the edge of the plate with a damp piece of paper towel. Refrigerate the cake briefly to let the icing harden. Then cut a checkerboard pattern in the icing on the top of the cake with a knife. Refrigerate until ready to serve. Then sprinkle lightly with cocoa powder shaken through a tea strainer. Serve at room temperature.

YIELD: 12 SERVINGS

Chocolate Icing

7 ounces semisweet chocolate
3 tablespoons unsalted butter
⅔ cup heavy cream

1. Melt the chocolate and butter over boiling water (see step 3 of previous recipe).
2. In a separate saucepan, bring the cream to a boil. Pour over melted butter and chocolate and beat vigorously with a whisk to produce a smooth icing. Immediately begin applying the icing to the top of the cake. While the icing is hot it is pourable and will spread with glassy smoothness over the top of the cake if you tilt the plate back and forth until the top is completely covered. To coat the sides, you will have to wait until the icing cools and stiffens so that it no longer drips but is still spreadable. If it cools too much and gets hard to spread, reheat gently in a double boiler and try again. Reheated icing may lose some of its gloss, but since you will be working on the sides of the cake this is not terribly important.

Carrot Cake

This is not a health-food recipe. It won't hurt you, of course, but it will fool most people who haven't experienced a good carrot cake before and won't be able to identify the basic ingredient. The icing is optional, but if you do use it, you will learn how to apply a (semi)solid icing once and for all. Apart from adding its taste and texture to a cake, an icing also helps to seal in moisture and freshness.

> 1½ pounds carrots, peeled (see page 44)
> 1 cup blanched almonds
> 1½ cups corn oil
> 2 cups sugar
> 4 eggs
> 1 teaspoon salt
> 1 teaspoon ground cinnamon
> 2 cups flour
> 2 teaspoons baking soda
> 1 recipe cream cheese icing (optional; see below)

1. Grease the inside of a 10-inch tube cake pan (see page 70). These pans, with their central tube, are universally available and cheap.

2. Preheat oven to 325 degrees.

3. Grate the carrots with the perforated grating disk of your processor or by hand, by rubbing the carrot against the fine teeth of a hand grater.

4. Chop the almonds finely by rocking the knife (see page 43). (You can also buy unblanched almonds and blanch them yourself. This saves money but not time and adds nothing to the taste of the ultimate product. To blanch: Boil the almonds briefly in plenty of water. Then pop off the loosened skins with your fingers. Spread the skinned nuts on a cookie sheet and put in a medium oven until they begin to brown. Remove and cool.)

5. In a large bowl, combine the oil and sugar and stir until blended with a wooden spoon. Add the eggs and beat until thoroughly mixed in.

6. In another bowl, stir together the salt, cinnamon, flour and baking soda so that they are well mixed. The baking soda (not baking powder) is a raising agent: Oven heat activates it, whereupon it aerates the cake and makes it light.

7. Stir the dry ingredients into the egg mixture. Blend thoroughly. Then stir in the carrots and almonds.

8. Pour the batter into the tube pan. Bake on a cookie sheet for 1¼ hours, on a rack positioned a third of the way up from the oven bottom. The cake is done when a toothpick or trussing needle inserted in the center comes out clean.

9. Let cool on a pastry rack. Then, run a knife around the edges of the cake. Set an inverted serving plate on top of the pan. With one hand on the plate and the other on the bottom of the pan, turn the cake over and set it down, with the plate now on the bottom. The cake should slide out as you raise the pan off the plate. If it doesn't, rap the bottom of the pan firmly and try again.

10. With an icing spatula or a dinner knife, spread icing on all exposed surfaces of the cake, including the center hole. Refrigerate until the beginning of the meal.

Cream Cheese Icing

8 ounces cream cheese
4 tablespoons unsalted butter, melted
2 tablespoons vanilla extract
1 1-pound box confectioners' sugar

1. Beat the cream cheese with an electric mixer until fluffy. This can be done by hand with a whisk, but you will regret the experience and gain nothing by it. A manual rotary mixer is a good

compromise if you aren't ready to invest in an electric mixer.

2. Add the butter and the vanilla, and then add the sugar gradually. Confectioners' sugar is sometimes called powdered sugar. It is very fine and has cornstarch added to it.

Angel Food Cake

White, light and pure, angel food cake is somewhat tricky, but it is the most elegant of traditional American cakes and worth the finicking. Unless you have a very strong right arm, don't attempt this without at least a portable electric mixer. Whisking a dozen egg whites to stiff peaks manually is no game. Like the carrot cake above, angel food cake is baked in a tube pan, but it is easier to unmold if the pan has a removable bottom and "feet" on the upper rim. I do not believe in icing angel food cakes. They are perfect by themselves, served with a puree of berries.

> 1 cup cake flour (an especially fine flour sold in boxes in any supermarket. Do not buy the "self-rising" variety.)
>
> 1½ cups sugar
>
> 12 egg whites (about 2 cups; see page 41 for basic instructions on separation. Since the quantity here is so large and the risk of contaminating many whites with a speck of yolk is great, it is prudent to set aside one bowl into which you separate one white at a time and another in which you collect the separated whites.)
>
> 1½ teaspoons cream of tartar (a powder derived from wine-making that stabilizes beaten whites)
>
> 1 teaspoon almond extract
>
> ¼ teaspoon salt
>
> 1 package frozen strawberries
>
> 1 package frozen raspberries

1. Preheat oven to 375 degrees. Set an oven rack a third of the way up from the bottom of the oven so that the large pan will be centered in the baking space. Put a cookie sheet on the rack.

2. In a mixing bowl, stir together the flour and ¾ cup sugar until very well mixed.

3. Whatever method you use to beat the egg whites, start slowly. When the mixture turns foamy, add cream of tartar, almond extract and salt. Begin beating again and, after the new ingredients have been incorporated, pour in the remaining ¾ cup sugar gradually. Keep on beating, at high speed now, until the egg whites leave stiff, moist peaks. This means that when you remove the whisk or the beaters, the whites hold their shape, perhaps drooping slightly, but they no longer slide around in the bowl. With an electric beater, you run the risk of overbeating, which produces dry, crumbly whites that don't hold air very well. Cure this by beating in a fresh white.

4. Fold the flour-sugar mixture into the whites. This and the rest of the recipe should be done without pause so that the whites don't sag from waiting. Folding is a gentle method of mixing. Take a third or so of the flour-sugar mixture and put it gently on top of the whites. Now cut into the whites with a rubber spatula and turn them over on top of the flour-sugar. Repeat this maneuver, rotating the bowl, until you don't see any unmixed dry ingredients. Then, repeat with half of the remaining flour-sugar and, after that's mixed in, with what is left.

5. Pour the batter into the ungreased tube pan, distributing it evenly. Use a rubber spatula so that you get all the batter. Cut through the batter in several places to eliminate large air pockets. Smooth the top of the batter and place the tube pan in the oven. Bake for 40 minutes. The cake is done when a knife inserted into it comes out clean. Also, the cake should spring back when pressed.

6. Cool as follows: Invert the pan and let it sit on its feet, if it has them. If not, hang it on a bottle neck inserted through the center hole.

7. Run a long knife or icing spatula around the outer and inner sides of the cake, separating it from the pan without tearing

it. If the pan has a removable bottom, you can just lift the cake out by holding on to the tube. Otherwise, work it loose by pressing the bottom of the cake loose with your fingers or an icing spatula. This is possible because an angel food cake is so springy and will regain its shape once you've pried it loose and set it on a serving platter.

8. In a blender or processor, puree the strawberries and raspberries together. They are frozen in sugar syrup and therefore make a lovely sweet sauce without further ado.

9. To serve, cut the cake with a serrated knife. Pour sauce over each piece.

Chocolate Mousse/Chocolate Soufflé

With the same ingredients and almost exactly the same method, you can make both of these famous French desserts. A mousse is a very refined sort of pudding. A soufflé is an airy, hot miracle that rises in the oven but collapses if you don't serve it immediately. You will want to make the mousse when you can work ahead of time; it has to be refrigerated several hours or overnight. The soufflé must be whipped together, literally, at the last minute and put in the oven after you've cleared the main course. Yes, this is a bit of a stunt, but it is easier than it sounds and will impress all but the most jaded. You will need to get a soufflé mold that holds 1 quart (4 cups). They come in various styles. Most of them are heavy circular ceramic bowls with flat bottoms. You can also use a charlotte mold, which is a tin container whose official purpose is, as the name implies, to act as a mold for those fancy ladyfinger concoctions called charlottes. Some day you might want to try one, and if you've already bought a charlotte mold to make soufflés, you're in business. Charlotte molds are also nice for rice puddings.

Don't attempt to substitute other flavorings for the chocolate in this recipe. Most soufflés are held together with a form of white sauce or béchamel. Chocolate acts as a binder all by itself, whence the radical simplicity of the recipe. Notice that the three main ingredients all come in quantities of 4. Memorize them and a few simple steps and you can make *mousse au chocolat* anywhere, without a recipe in front of you. People who can do that become legends in their own time.

> 4 ounces sweet chocolate (buy premium imported chocolate if possible)
> 4 eggs, separated (see page 41)
> 4 tablespoons (½ stick) unsalted butter
> Confectioners' sugar (for soufflé)

1. Break the chocolate into pieces and put it in a saucepan. Cover it with hot water and let it stand until it softens to the point where a knife will cut it easily. This takes only a couple of minutes. It is an extremely convenient method taught to me by Richard Grausman, the Cordon Bleu chef and cooking teacher. As soon as you see the chocolate beginning to melt visibly into the water, you are done. Pour off the water. Only a smidgen of chocolate will be lost.

2. Then, immediately, whisk the yolks into the chocolate completely, until there are no streaks of lighter color.

3. If making the soufflé, preheat oven to 475 degrees. Grease the inside of the mold (see page 70) and then drop a handful of plain sugar into it. Rotate the mold so that the entire inner surface is coated (the sugar will stick to the butter). Dump out excess sugar. Set mold aside.

4. Add butter to the mixture from step 2 and stir over low heat until the butter melts. Be careful here. If you let more than the most gentle heat penetrate the mixture, you risk scrambling the egg yolks. Therefore, stir vigorously, and if your pan is lightweight (tsk, tsk), either hold it an inch or so off the burner or do this step with the pan immersed in simmering water.

5. Pour mixture into a bowl. Set aside.

6. Beat the egg whites until they hold soft peaks (see page 85).

7. Knock off the egg white sticking to the whisk or beaters into the chocolate mixture. Stir until well blended. This lightens the mixture and makes it easier to fold in the rest of the whites without deflating them.

8. With a rubber spatula, scrape the rest of the whites into the bowl with the chocolate mixture. Fold in (see page 85).

9. If making the mousse, scrape the mixture into a glass bowl or other serving dish, cover with plastic wrap and refrigerate several hours or overnight. When the mousse has set, it is ready to serve. You should remove it from the refrigerator midway through the meal so that it isn't ice cold.

10. For soufflé, scrape the mixture into the prepared mold and set in the center of the oven over a cookie sheet. Bake for a couple of minutes, just long enough for the top of the soufflé to set and for a little rising to take place. If you have to open the oven door to determine this, don't worry. Just close it and reduce the temperature to 425 degrees. Bake another 6 minutes, until the exterior is firm. The soufflé will have risen nicely and the center will still be soft.

11. Remove carefully from oven. Dust with confectioners' sugar. For this, a simple strainer will suffice, as will a flour sifter. Serve the soufflé immediately. "Carve" it with two large spoons. The soft center makes a "sauce" for the firmer outer pieces.

YIELD: 6 SERVINGS

Two Classic Confections

Sugar changes its nature several times as you heat it from room temperature to 350 degrees, at which point it burns. In between, its crystal structure alters as the heat rises. Candymakers have learned to take advantage of these changes, and by keeping careful track of the temperature of their sugar, they are able to produce soft, hard, grainy, glassy and caramelized sugar confections. You can do the same, but you had better be prepared to play by the book. Sugar cookery is a close-tolerance business.

The first step is to get yourself a candy thermometer. There are ways of determining the temperature of hot sugar by dropping a bit of it in ice water and then scrutinizing whether it makes a soft ball or hard ball, and so forth. But I think that this old-fashioned method will lead to much failure—of the heart as well as the fudge.

A candy thermometer is calibrated to mark the various crucial temperatures. It will have a clip on it so that you can leave it attached to the pan while the sugar cooks (dipping it in and out tends to cause drips to fall back into the sugar, which promotes unwanted crystal growth). A candy thermometer can also be used to measure the temperature of hot oil for deep frying.

Nut Brittle

This is the best candy in the standard American repertory. Anyone can succeed with brittle the first time. That is why it has always been a favorite rainy-day project for children. Adults too will enjoy the moment when the nut mixture foams up in the pan from contact with the baking soda. It is also amusing to pour the whole batch out of the pan.

Oil
3 ounces unsalted nuts (see note)
¼ teaspoon baking soda
½ cup sugar
1 ounce (2 tablespoons) unsalted butter

1. Using a piece of paper towel, spread vegetable oil on a cookie sheet and set aside.

2. Chop the nuts with a chef's knife on a cutting board (see page 43). Pour into a small bowl, sprinkle with the baking soda and stir.

4. Pour ¼ cup water and the sugar into a heavy-bottomed saucepan and place over low heat. Let the sugar dissolve. Add the butter, raise heat to medium and boil the mixture until it registers 280 degrees on the candy thermometer, the soft-crack stage.

5. Remove from heat, immediately add nuts, and stir for a moment, while the baking soda goes to work and makes the mixture foam up. But do not overdo this, because you could beat out all the air and get a dense brittle. Pour the mixture onto the prepared cookie sheet. Set aside to cool and harden. Break into pieces.

NOTE: Unsalted nuts may be found at health-food stores. If only salted nuts are available, toss and roll them first in a dry towel, then in a damp towel. Spread them in a thin layer on a cookie sheet to dry for a few hours.

Chocolate Fudge

2 cups less 2 tablespoons milk
4 cups sugar
¼ teaspoon salt
4 ounces semisweet chocolate (a specific type of baking chocolate sold in the baking sections of supermarkets), grated by hand on the medium panel of a

    metal grater, so that it will melt quickly
6 tablespoons (¾ stick) butter, cut into pats
1 teaspoon vanilla extract

1. In a large saucepan, bring the milk to a boil. Milk will foam up like a volcano and erupt over the sides of the pan if you let it continue to boil, so don't leave the room and do remove it from the heat as soon as it begins to foam up. While you wait, grease an 8 × 8 × 2-inch rectangular pan and set it aside (see page 70).

2. Add the sugar, salt and chocolate. Stir until everything solid has dissolved. Set over high heat, covered, and boil for a couple of minutes, so that steam will wash down any crystals left from the stirring. The mixture is now heavy enough to prevent the milk from foaming out of the pan.

3. Uncover, reduce heat slightly, attach candy thermometer and cook until the thermometer reads 238 degrees. Do not despair when the temperature seems to hover below 220 degrees for a great long time. This is a normal feature of sugar physics. Once it does reach 220, it will zip right along. Do not, in any case, stir the contents of the pan. This will ruin everything. Just stay alert until the sugar mixture reaches 238, the soft-ball stage. Then remove from heat, with as little shaking and sloshing as possible. None, in fact. Set the pan either in a sink or in a big pan filled with an inch or two of cold water. This will speed the cooling. Do not stir. Do not remove the thermometer.

4. When the mixture has cooled to 110 degrees, remove the thermometer and beat in the butter with a wooden spoon or a portable electric beater. After a few minutes of beating, add the vanilla and continue to beat until the future fudge loses its glossy shine and begins to get hard. When the drips from the spoon or the beaters hold their shape, pour into the greased pan to a depth of about ¾ inch. Don't worry if you haven't picked the ideal pan and need another one. You have time to grease another one quickly. Cut the fudge into squares before it cools completely and hardens.

YIELD: ABOUT 2½ POUNDS

Chocolate Chip Cookies

These are also called tollhouse cookies, because of their one-time association with the Toll House Inn in Whitman, Massachusetts. In recent years, franchisers and sidewalk peddlers have exploited the national craving for these classic cookies. Famous Amos and David, to name two chocolate-chip entrepreneurs, have put their personal stamp on a cookie that really needed no improvement.

For the record, chocolate-chip cookies are simple drop cookies made luxurious with bits of chocolate scattered through the dough. Drop cookies are so called because you form the individual cookie by dropping a spoonful of dough onto a baking sheet. Baking soda in the dough makes them puff out as they cook. In 10 minutes or so, they're done—crisp, not bendable like some of the gourmet variations on sale at our better food boutiques. If you want to rise above commercial, industrially uniform chocolate bits, buy premium-quality semisweet chocolate and cut it into little chunks yourself. Most people will think you've invented something, instead of re-creating the original. Also, the chocolate will probably be a better grade.

Some tips: Store cookies after they are completely cool in a plastic bag from which all the air has been squeezed out. Tie the bag and put it in a tightly sealed container. Soggy cookies can be revived in a 300-degree oven in a minute or three. If you find that cookies are overbrowning or burning on the bottoms before the rest of the cookie has finished baking, try double-panning: Nest a second baking sheet under the first. This may slightly increase the overall cooking time, but it will promote even cooking.

> 8 tablespoons (1 stick) butter, left unrefrigerated until soft
> ½ cup sugar
> ½ cup brown sugar
> 1 egg
> ½ teaspoon vanilla extract
> 1 cup plus 2 tablespoons flour

½ teaspoon salt

½ teaspoon baking soda

1 cup (12 ounces) semisweet chocolate morsels, or the same quantity of ordinary semisweet chocolate, chopped to whatever size and shape suits you

1 cup chopped walnuts (optional and, I think, an excessive addition, although it is often seen)

1. Preheat oven to 375 degrees. Grease a cookie sheet or two or three (see page 70), and set them aside.

2. Put the butter in a bowl and start beating it. This can certainly be done by hand, with a whisk or even a wooden spoon, but an electric mixer is the tool of choice. When the butter is creamed, i.e., beaten to a smooth smear, slightly aerated, and therefore more welcoming to other ingredients, beat in the white and brown sugars. This is the serious moment. Beat until very smooth. Then beat in the egg and vanilla and keep beating until the dough looks light.

3. In a small bowl, stir together the flour and salt. Put the baking soda in a coffee cup and moisten it with a small amount of hot water (stir to a paste or slurry; this starts to activate the baking soda).

4. Beat roughly half the flour mixture into the butter-sugar mixture. Then beat in the moistened soda. Then beat in the rest of the flour mixture. Beat until thoroughly blended and then stir in the chocolate (and chopped nuts, if you must).

5. Do not wait. Start dropping nuggets of dough onto the baking sheet. The standard amount to drop per cookie is a heaping teaspoonful. This means you use the teaspoon as a scoop and use whatever amount it pulls away from the mass of dough. Then you drop (fling) the dough onto the baking sheet. At this point, tradition divides between those who leave the little mounds alone and those who moisten their fingers and press them flat. This is not a trivial difference. It takes a bit longer to bake mounds than to bake thinner, flattened cookies. The outside of the mound will be a more intense brown, and the cookie itself will not be as crisp as a flat-

tened one. All in all, it seems to me worthwhile to do the flatten-ing. Either way, give the cookies room to expand, about 2 inches on all sides.

6. Bake for 10 minutes in the middle of the oven. Cookies are done if they are light brown. Take a metal spatula and move them from the sheet to a rack. Let cool. Cookies will be soft when they come out of the oven, but will get crisp after cooling.

Start another batch, continue as before and keep on going un-til you have used up all the dough. You can bake two or even three sheets at a time, but the lower sheet will cook faster than the one(s) above it. I don't recommend this. It adds complexity and danger without really speeding things up very much. You can, by the way, reuse a greased baking sheet without regreasing; just scrape off crumbs from the previous batch.

YIELD: ABOUT 50 COOKIES

Pears Poached in Red Wine

This is an embarrassingly simple French household standby. Nevertheless, it looks and is extremely elegant. The pears are meltingly soft, but lose nothing of their flavor. The wine tints them a delicate red-pink. They stand up on the plate, whole and with their stems still attached, but they are peeled and easy to eat. The poaching liquid, after being rapidly boiled down, serves as a sauce.

> 10 pears of any variety except the very small seckels, almost ripe but still firm and unblemished
> Juice of ½ lemon
> ½ cup sugar
> 2 cups red wine

1. Peel the pears: First cut away the small "button" at the end opposite the stem. Then peel as you would an apple (see page 75),

striving to leave the flesh as smooth as possible and with no trace of the knife. Leave the stem, but shorten it if it seems overlong. As you finish peeling each pear, put it in a bowl of cold water acidulated with the lemon juice. This prevents the flesh from oxidizing and turning brown.

2. In a pan just large enough to accommodate all the pears standing up, bring the sugar, wine and 1½ cups water to a boil. The sugar will dissolve in the liquid and make a syrup. Set the pears upright in the syrup, cover and reduce heat so that the syrup bubbles slowly. Cook for 15 minutes or until the pears are tender. Very slow boiling in a small amount of water is what is meant by the term *poach*. Shake the pan from time to time so that the pears don't stick to the bottom. When the pears are done, let them cool in their cooking liquid.

3. With a large spoon, gently remove the pears to a serving platter or to individual shallow bowls.

4. Raise the heat and let the syrup reduce (boil down), uncovered, to ⅔ cup. To determine exactly whether you have the right amount, pour the syrup into a measuring cup. If it is underreduced, pour it back and continue boiling. If it is overreduced, simply add water to bring it back to the correct quantity. You must not walk out on the syrup while it is reducing. It can boil away altogether and burn if you aren't on hand.

5. Pour syrup over pears and serve.

YIELD: 10 SERVINGS

NOTE: Under refrigeration, the cooked pears will keep quite nicely for a few days, as will the syrup. This dish can be made ahead. The quantity given may seem quite large, but, aside from the extra peeling, you will benefit from an economy of scale if you do it this way, especially when pears are in season. On the other hand, feel free to halve the recipe and cook it in a smaller pan just large enough to hold 5 pears.

4

BREAKFAST

BREAKFAST IS A STRICT RITUAL. THE LIST OF DISHES MOST
Americans normally eat for breakfast is very short, and this chapter will include most of them. But even if our conventional breakfast diet is highly restricted in its range, the meal itself need not
be meager, far from it. A full American breakfast is very full indeed, compared to the coffee and pastry that suffices for most of
Europe. We have inherited the heftier breakfast tradition of England and of our own pioneers, whose calorie needs were far greater
than ours.

Today, many people, facing up to the reality of their sedentary
lives, have trimmed back their everyday breakfasts to a Spartan
regimen of juice, coffee and toast. This is my normal pattern, but
on weekends I love to backslide and wallow in the luxury of old-
fashioned breakfast foods: pancakes and waffles and eggs cooked
every which way with bacon or sausage.

Breakfast, then, involves a short yet sumptuous list of recipes.
Breakfast, moreover, is the only time when most of us eat these
dishes. They are as culturally marked for the morning as a dinner
jacket is for after six. People who eat pancakes for lunch or scrambled eggs for dinner are distorting the shape of normal life and
letting what the poet Wallace Stevens in "Sunday Morning" called
"Complacencies of the peignoir, and late coffee and oranges" spread
like the drowsiness of dawn over the whole day.

But there is nothing slack or sleepy-eyed about breakfast for
the person cooking it. Since so many things must be timed to appear together, often more than once in the course of a single breakfast
as more and more people emerge from their nightly cocoons, vig-
ilance and concentration are essential.

Coffee

Coffee has inspired many myths and cult practices. At one extreme palpitates the coffee fetishist with his costly (and probably counterfeit) Jamaican Blue Mountain beans, which he buys raw, roasts himself, grinds himself and brews in a device that would look more at home in a lab.

I will not dispute that good coffee is better than bad coffee. I once had dinner in the home of a Brazilian coffee exporter, and I will never forget the aroma of the coffee he served.

But as a practical daily matter, I find myself quite content to buy dark-roasted Cuban-style coffee (El Pico, Bustelo) already ground and in cans, and to brew it by almost any method that isn't percolation or that does not take place in an automatic machine of the type popular in offices.

If your preference in coffee is for a more standard American roast, then life is truly simple. Buy whatever the supermarket supplies, measure two tablespoons per six-ounce cup and brew it with water that has cooled slightly after coming to a boil. And keep the pot scrupulously clean. Most truly bad coffee is made in old pots that have picked up unpleasant tastes from previous brewings.

Coffee must not boil. It is always worse after reheating. Keep it in a thermos if you want to have it around all day.

Orange Juice

We drink undiluted orange juice at breakfast for two related reasons. America in a normal year grows a large crop of inexpensive oranges. When this first began to happen several decades ago, a clever publicist, Edward Bernays, persuaded nearly everyone his ads could reach that orange juice was an essential component of a healthy diet and that it kicked off a hearty breakfast ideally well.

If you care about the taste of orange juice, there is only one way to go. Squeeze your own from juice oranges (not eating oranges) just before drinking it. Freshly squeezed orange juice goes "stale," even in the refrigerator, after a few hours. If you don't believe this, squeeze some, let it sit overnight and taste it against freshly squeezed juice the next morning.

To my taste, the best store-bought orange juice made from concentrate is always inferior to fresh-squeezed juice from whole oranges. Frozen juice is third in line in quality.

Eggs

Freshness is all, or almost all. An egg shows its age long before it spoils altogether and gives off a telltale sulfurous odor. Old eggs have whites that turn cheesy when heated. They have less flavor. And they crack on contact with boiling water because such a large air bubble has accumulated inside the shell.

Look at the dates on egg cartons. Buy the newest ones you can. Also, look inside the carton to check for broken shells. Rotate each egg. If any stick, they are probably broken underneath; hidden seepage has made them adhere to the carton.

Use eggs as soon as you can after purchase. While they wait for you, keep them refrigerated. Cold slows down their deterioration dramatically.

Scrambled Eggs

Even noncooks tend to be able to produce scrambled eggs after a fashion. Actually, there is a fair degree of finesse involved in turning out smooth, moist scrambled eggs. The idea is to control the coagulation or scrambling of the yolks through slow cooking and careful manipulation of the egg mass. Done well, scrambled eggs can be elegant. And, if you make them, you control the exquisite range of possibilities from small to large curd.

5–6 eggs
Salt
Pepper
2–4 tablespoons butter, cut into pats

1. Crack the eggs into a bowl. Add salt and pepper. Beat until well mixed with a small whisk or a nonsilver fork (egg tarnishes silver).

2. In a small skillet, melt the butter over medium heat until it foams and the foam subsides.

3. Reduce heat to medium low. Pour egg mixture into skillet. Do not leave the room.

4. Depending on the thickness of the skillet and the temperature of your eggs, in a minute or two or three, the eggs should begin to coagulate. Test this by scraping them away from the skillet every now and then.

5. Continue scraping and stirring the egg mixture until it has almost completely dried out, or until it has dried out almost as much as you would like it to (cooking will continue even after you remove the skillet from the stove, because heat will continue to radiate from the skillet itself).

The faster you scrape and stir, the more uniform a texture you will achieve. This result is called small curd. If, on the other hand, you hang back and let a bit more of the egg adhere to the skillet between passes with the spatula, you will get large curds.

It is also possible to vary the basic consistency of scrambled eggs either by mixing in a bit of milk at the beginning, to lighten the eggs, or by using extra butter (see ingredient list).

6. Scrape onto a serving platter and serve immediately.

YIELD: 2 SERVINGS

VARIATIONS: To dress up scrambled eggs, add any of the following with the eggs in step 3 above: ¼ pound smoked salmon or 6 slices salami, roughly chopped; 12 cooked asparagus tips (see page 133 for cooking instructions).

Fried Eggs

The legendary French chef Fernand Point taught his apprentices how to fry eggs as their first lesson in cooking. To impress upon them the delicacy of the process, he made them hold the skillet over a candle until its heat caused the whites to turn opaque.

2 tablespoons butter
4 eggs

1. Melt the butter over medium heat in a 10-inch skillet. It will foam soon after it has melted. Very shortly after that, the foam will subside, signifying that the water originally contained in the butter has boiled off and that it is now ready for frying.

2. Lower the heat as far as possible. Then, quickly crack the eggs into the butter. Do this by rapping the egg against the skillet's edge and then opening the shell so that the egg will pour into the butter. Take pains to aim each egg over a fresh area of the skillet. Each egg should cook separately. If they do happen to coalesce, you can easily reseparate them after they have cooked by cutting through the whites with the edge of a metal spatula.

3. The eggs are done as soon as the whites turn opaque. If you wait a minute or so after this point, the yolk will thicken slightly. Either way, you have eggs done sunny-side up. Slide a metal spatula under each egg, lift them one at a time and slide them onto individual plates.

4. To satisfy folks who detest runny yolks and insist on having their eggs "over," you must wait until the yolks have thickened (as in step 3) and then flip them over in the pan with a metal spatula. Should the yolk smash on contact, relax: It will cook anyway and the mistake will be invisible.

Boiled Eggs

Avoid doing this with any but the newest eggs.

Aside from freshness, the key here is timing, as you know from years of receiving soft-boiled eggs that are either hard or almost raw. This is an area where nearly everyone is a vocal connoisseur. Ask people to describe how they like their eggs, not how many minutes they cook them. They may think that the perfect runny egg takes three minutes of immersion in simmering water, but the white of a three-minute egg will be unappetizingly clear if the egg is ice cold to start with or if it is a jumbo.

1. The most reliable method is to start with (unshelled) room-temperature eggs and cold water. Put the eggs in a pan and cover with the water.

2. Set over high heat and bring to a boil. Lower heat and simmer. Three minutes should produce a runny egg with an opaque but loose white. Four minutes will turn the white solid and the yolk thickish but not yet solid. More cooking than this yields an egg you might as well call hard-boiled. Actually, for true hard-boiled eggs, cook 15 minutes. In all the above cases, you can add roughly 2 minutes of cooking time for refrigerated eggs and add 1 minute or so for jumbos.

3. After the cooking time has elapsed, immediately run the eggs under cold water to stop further cooking. This also makes it practical to handle soft-boiled eggs and shell them. Just don't overdo it. A few seconds should lower the shell temperature without chilling the interior.

NOTE: To shell hard-boiled eggs, rap the middle of the shell gently against the edge of a table. Keep doing this, while rotating the egg, until you have produced a circular crack around the egg at its equator. Then set the egg on the counter, on its side. With the flat of your hand, roll the egg back and forth a few times, pressing on it lightly. This separates the shell from the egg and makes it easy to pull off the shell in a few large pieces. Cold hard-boiled eggs are a standard option for breakfast at French cafés (and are not a bad thing to consider for your own breakfast, since they can be kept for several days and are instantly available when you are in a rush in the morning).

Poached Eggs

To poach is to cook something in water just below the boiling point. In other words, it is very gentle cooking, ideal for boiling eggs outside the shell without roiling them apart or for fish that a full boil would disintegrate. It is not well known that poached eggs can be prepared in advance, held and served at your convenience without any loss of quality.

> **Vinegar**
> **Salt**
> 8 **jumbo eggs**
> 4 **English muffins, halved with a fork (see page 106), or 8 slices of white bread**

1. Fill a large skillet with water to a depth of 1½ to 2 inches. Measure the water as you pour it in. Add 1 tablespoon vinegar and 1 teaspoon salt per quart of water.

2. Bring the water to a full boil. Break the eggs gently into the water. Lower heat until the water barely trembles. Cook for about 3 minutes or until the egg whites have solidified just enough to permit the eggs to be lifted out of the water with a slotted spoon or slotted metal spatula and set in a pan of cold water. This stops the cooking immediately.

3. Trim ragged edges of the whites with scissors while the eggs are still in the water bath. You can leave the eggs in the water bath for an hour or so, until you are ready to reheat them.

4. Toast the English muffins or the bread slices. Keep warm in a 200-degree oven.

5. Heat a pan of water to 120 degrees, slightly cooler than hot tap water. You can test with a thermometer to be absolutely sure. This temperature is just hot enough to heat the eggs but not so hot that it overcooks the yolks before you have a chance to remove and serve them.

6. Slide in the eggs. As soon as they have heated through—test this by lifting one and touching it carefully—lift them out with a slotted spoon and set them on the muffin halves or toasted bread slices and serve immediately. Another popular way to serve poached eggs is eggs Benedict: Immediately after the eggs are finished cooking, set them on top of split oven-warmed English muffins (one egg per muffin half) and bathe with **hollandaise sauce** (see page 238).

YIELD: 6 SERVINGS

Toast and Muffins

The modern toaster oven not only functions as an economical auxiliary oven but is a significant improvement on the pop-up toaster, which itself improved on oven or broiler toasting. The pop-up toaster brought precision timing and automation to toasting; the toaster oven added a larger space and a larger opening. So with a toaster oven you can toast 4 slices of bread at once or you can easily toast bagels (or other thick breads and rolls) that never quite fit into a toaster's slots. All you need to know is how to slice the bagel. This isn't much different from slicing bread. All you need is the right knife and a steady hand.

A good bread-slicing knife should have a long blade, ideal for making straight slices. It also has to bite easily into crusts. I prefer a good-quality serrated knife for this job. Each scallop of the blade acts like a saw tooth. You just line up the blade and cut straight down. With a little practice, you'll be able to slice an entire loaf into perfect ¼-inch slices. To slice a bagel, set it down flat and hold it steady with one hand. Turn the knife on its side and slice through halfway. Then stand the bagel up and cut through the rest of the way.

For English muffins that have not already been sliced at the bakery, you should use a fork instead of a knife. Perforate the muffin all the way around by punching the fork tines into the side of the muffin. Then pull apart gently. The texture inside will be classically rough, not flattened out the way a knife would make it.

French Toast

This is a recipe meant to salvage slightly stale bread, but it works very nicely with fresh bread and is particularly appealing with the braided Jewish Sabbath loaf, called *challah*.

    ½ **cup milk**
    2 **eggs, lightly beaten**
    2 **tablespoons butter**
    4 **slices bread**

1. Stir the milk and eggs together until well blended.
2. Melt the butter in a large, heavy skillet over medium heat.
3. Dip the bread in the milk-egg mixture, coating both sides. Let excess drip off and then put the bread in the skillet.
4. Brown lightly on both sides. Use tongs or a metal spatula to turn.
5. Serve immediately with maple syrup or confectioners' sugar.

YIELD: 4 SLICES FRENCH TOAST

Cinnamon Toast

There is no more comforting food than raisin toast topped with buttery cinnamon. You probably knew that already from sublime experience. Read on and you'll see how easy it is to satisfy your yen for this breakfast treat anytime.

2 tablespoons butter at room temperature
1½ teaspoons ground cinnamon
5 tablespoons light-brown sugar
3–4 slices raisin bread

1. In a bowl, mash the butter together with the cinnamon and light brown sugar.
2. Spread thinly over one side of each slice of bread.
3. Toast in a toaster oven or place under a regular oven broiler. Put foil under the toast to catch any runs from the cinnamon-butter mixture.

YIELD: 3–4 SLICES CINNAMON TOAST

Fried Bread

When you have finished cooking **bacon** (see page 108), instead of throwing away the drippings or keeping them for a rainy day, leave them in the skillet and, while they are still very hot, slip one piece of bread at a time into the fat and fry until well browned. This may not be the world's healthiest dish, but it is certainly delicious. Be warned: The drippings will fry the bread very quickly if they are truly hot. Be ready with tongs or a spatula and remove the bread before it burns. Then add another piece right away and continue until your appetite or the drippings are gone. Drain fried bread on paper toweling.

Bacon and Sausage

Bacon

American bacon is meatier than similar cuts in other countries. It is smoked, and it usually comes presliced. Some country bacon is sold in slabs and you have to slice it yourself, which is tricky, but the taste is sometimes superior to presliced packinghouse bacon.

Since bacon is very fatty, it requires no extra fat for cooking. Just lay individual slices in a skillet as close together as you can arrange them. They will shrink dramatically during cooking. A 12-inch skillet should hold ½ pound with perhaps some overlapping. Cooked bacon can be held in a warming oven while a second batch cooks.

Set the skillet over medium heat. Soon the fat will begin to render out of the bacon. When it sizzles, cooking has begun. Keep an eye on things, and peek from time to time at the bottom of the strips. When they have browned, turn them with tongs. They should be fully cooked shortly after you turn them. Remove as soon as finished and drain on paper toweling.

Sausage

Breakfast sausage comes in two forms: as links (in casings, like frankfurters), or as patties (a loose mixture of ground pork and other ingredients).

To cook link sausages: Fill a skillet to a depth of ½ inch with water. Bring to a boil. Meanwhile, prick the sausages in many places with a fork. This keeps the links from bursting and lets some of the fat out while the water is boiling away. Then the sausages can brown in their own fat. The water prevents the sausages from burning until they heat up and yield enough fat for frying.

When the water boils, put in the sausages. After the water

boils away, the fat will sizzle and the cooking temperature in the skillet will rise sharply. If fat starts to smoke, lower heat slightly. Cook until the sausages are well browned on all sides (keep turning them until this happens) and cooked through. Test by cutting into one. Pink raw sausage is undesirable and possibly unhealthy.

TO COOK PATTIES: Form the meat into half-dollar–size patties or just slice it off the roll, if it is sold that way. There is no need to add more than a film of extra bacon drippings, lard or oil to the pan, since the sausage meat has plenty of its own. Arrange in a skillet and set over medium heat. When you hear fat begin to sizzle, raise heat slightly. Cook thoroughly, turning once. Both sides should be crisply browned.

Quick Breads

Muffins, pancakes and waffles all fall into this category. They are rapid-fire recipes for exploiting flour. Prepared mixes for all of them are widely sold, but I have never understood their appeal, since quick breads are so quick. Also, by making them from scratch you save money, you use fresh, natural ingredients and you probably end up consuming less sugar.

Bran Muffins with Raisins

Commercial bran muffins are no picnic. They taste dry and mass-produced, which, of course, they are. People eat them anyway, often because bran is physiologically useful in promoting bowel regularity and putting roughage into a diet. This recipe will accomplish all that, but the muffins it produces are also moist and appealing to eat. You will be surprised at how easy it is to whip up a batch in the morning. Muffins are quick bread, remember.

4 teaspoons baking powder
½ teaspoon salt
¾ cup flour
1 cup bran
½ cup raisins
2 tablespoons sugar
½ cup milk
1 egg, lightly beaten
2 tablespoons butter, melted

1. Grease a muffin tin and preheat oven to 400 degrees.

2. In a mixing bowl, stir together baking power, salt, flour, bran, raisins and sugar. Then stir in the milk, egg and melted butter, gradually, but do not beat longer than necessary to blend ingredients. Overbeating leads to toughness.

3. Fill the containers of the muffin tin to ⅔ their depth. Bake for 30 minutes or until the muffins begin to pull away from the sides of the tin and are no longer moist inside.

YIELD: ABOUT 10 MUFFINS

Corn Muffins

This is a traditional Southern corn-muffin recipe. Note that it does not call for sugar. You can certainly add a couple of tablespoons to the batter in step 2, but why not opt for austerity and add the sweetness with jam later on? I am not specifying yellow or white cornmeal. Yellow will give you a yellow muffin. Different grades of milling will produce different crumbs. They are all good in my opinion.

1 cup cornmeal
1 cup flour
½ teaspoon salt

4 teaspoons baking powder
1 cup milk
1 egg, lightly beaten
2 tablespoons butter, melted

1. Grease a muffin tin and preheat the oven to 400 degrees.

2. In a mixing bowl, combine the cornmeal, flour, salt and baking power. Stir together thoroughly.

3. Beat in the milk, gradually, and then the egg and melted butter. Stir just enough to moisten the dry ingredients and to work the liquid into the dough. Muffins are quick bread; overworking them does not help and can turn them into stone.

4. Spoon the dough into the compartments of the muffin tin. Fill each one to about two thirds of its depth. Bake for 25 minutes or until the muffins begin to pull away from the sides of the tin and are no longer moist inside.

YIELD: ABOUT 10 MUFFINS

Waffles

Waffle batter is greatly similar to the batter for other quick breads. But instead of being cooked in a tin or free form on a hot metal surface, waffles are baked in gridded, two-sided waffle irons that confine the batter in thin sheets while they cook, and impress on them the traditional checkerboard pattern of recessed squares. Irons come in two varieties. Electric wafflers maintain an ideal temperature. You grease them, pour on the batter, close the iron and cook until done. The second variety, a modern version of the pre-electric original, is a hinged iron that has to be heated over a stove burner. They both come with temperature gauges and fancy recipes. They will also cook nonyeast-raised waffles of the type that follows, which millions of Americans have always devoured with enthusiasm and maple syrup.

1½ cups flour
½ teaspoon salt
1 tablespoon baking powder
1 tablespoon sugar
1 cup milk
2 eggs, lightly beaten
1 tablespoon butter, melted

1. Lightly grease and preheat a waffle iron to the point recommended by the manufacturer.

2. Stir together the flour, salt, baking powder and sugar.

3. Stir in milk, eggs and melted butter until the batter is smooth. Do not overbeat or the waffles will be leathery.

4. Pour batter onto the iron, leaving an inch or so at the edge. Close the iron and bake approximately 5 minutes. Repeat until all the batter has been used up.

YIELD: 4–5 WAFFLES

Pancakes

These are standard American pancakes. They are not crepes or blinis or *pfannkuchen*. They are not particularly thin or delicate, but they are extremely easy to make and taste delicious in the morning with maple syrup.

2¼ cups all-purpose flour
1 tablespoon plus ½ teaspoon baking powder
1 teaspoon salt
1 tablespoon sugar
2 eggs, lightly beaten
1¼ cups milk
4 tablespoons butter, melted

1. Stir together the flour, baking powder, salt and sugar in a mixing bowl.

2. Stir the egg, milk and melted butter into the flour mixture, working only until the batter is thoroughly moistened. Vigorous beating will produce leaden pancakes.

3. Lightly grease and heat a heavy griddle or skillet.

4. Drop the batter onto the cooking surface from a large kitchen spoon. The capacity of the spoon will determine the size of the pancake, but this is not a terribly crucial matter. If you want bigger or smaller pancakes, then adjust on the second try. For very large ones, dip a teacup into the batter and pour it out onto the griddle or skillet. At any rate, you can cook as many pancakes of whatever size you like at one time. The only limit is the size of the cooking surface and your ability to attend to them all.

If the batter from one pancake should spread and merge with a neighbor, cut them apart with a spatula after they have set. You will rapidly get the hang of pouring out very similar circular pancakes one after the other.

This is an assembly-line operation. The cook does not generally get to eat pancakes until the last batch is finished. It is possible to hold pancakes in stacks in a warming oven, but they do not improve with time.

It is difficult to specify a cooking heat. Be prepared to sacrifice the first pancake. Even experienced pancake cooks need to adjust the heat and "set" the pan each time they get started. Try medium-high heat to begin. Pancakes cook very quickly. When they have begun to bubble on top, turn and cook until done. (This is a matter of taste, to a certain extent, and will also depend on the thickness of the batter. Most people want pancakes browned on both sides and cooked right through. You should probably peek at the bottom of the first few and even cut into one or two just to reassure yourself that all is going well.)

YIELD: ABOUT 18 PANCAKES

5

GOING IT ALONE: COOKING FOR ONE

I LIKE TO COOK FOR ME. ME ALONE. NOT EVERY DAY OR EVEN often, but when the occasion arrives that I am my only guest for dinner, I know that I can eat exactly what I want in the way that I want it. I can prepare foods that my family won't willingly consume but which I particularly crave. (Kidneys are the leading example.) I can season my way (vigorously), dispense with napkins and eat standing up at the counter. You, no doubt, have your own personal menu and style, your own odd manners and proclivities— or you will discover them as you embark on solo voyages in the kitchen. Cooking for oneself is a small but delicious adventure, entirely different from eating alone the food left or sent or packaged by others.

Some people, perhaps most, find eating alone a quick route to depression or to undisciplined gorging. Once, when my wife was away on a working trip, I sustained myself entirely on a gift box of chocolate and coffee. Never again.

There are two healthy approaches to solitary feeding: quantity or speed. If you are steadily by yourself, it may suit you to cook two or three main dishes intended for four people or more, freeze them in several small containers and alternate them, defrosting a different one each day for two weeks. Do the cooking all at once when you have the time, on a Sunday afternoon for instance. You will have to choose dishes that keep—stews and soups and such. But this stockpile will ensure that you are never without reasonable meals. And you can compensate for the relative narrowness of the menus and space their repetition by interleaving foods that can be prepared easily at the last minute—chops, steaks, fish. Another advantage of the quantity approach is that it can be adapted to the sudden arrival of others. And the cooking involved is the same as what you would do ordinarily for a group; it requires no special strategies of marketing or recipe choice, as long as you have picked dishes that keep.

The speed approach is the one, however, that most single or solo cooks will choose most frequently. It allows the maximum freedom and does not entail advance planning or storage or the feat of morning alertness defrosting obliges.

Since the quantity approach does not involve cooking that is in any way different from ordinary cooking for groups, this chapter will concern itself exclusively with speed menus tailored for one person. Thousands of dishes fall into this category, which French restaurants refer to as *cuisine à la minute*. The recipes here have been chosen to represent basic techniques that can be applied to a large variety of similar foods. Frying fish fillets is almost always the same job, whether you have cod or salmon. Once you can sauté a lamb chop, you can tackle pork chops in virtually the same way. And so on.

These basic techniques can, of course, be extended to more than a single chop, more than one portion of asparagus. But speed cookery is the ideal place to start if you are on your own. Fasten your apron strings.

Hamburger

Even if you never make more than one of these at a time, buy at least a pound of ground meat and divide it into 4 equal parts; then freeze each in a plastic bag. In the morning, take out a package and leave it on the counter to defrost.

¼ pound ground beef chuck

1. Form the meat into a patty.
2. Heat a small skillet over high heat. Add the patty. When

the underside has browned to your satisfaction, turn it over with a spatula and brown the other side.

3. Lower heat to medium and continue cooking until patty is done. Check by cutting into it at the thickest point.

YIELD: 1 HAMBURGER

Sautéed Chops

2 chops, lamb, veal or pork (if the veal chops are running very large, then use only one)
Salt
Pepper
2 tablespoons butter
½ cup heavy cream (optional)

1. Rub the chops on both sides with the salt and pepper. Go easy.

2. Melt the butter over medium heat in a skillet and heat until the foam subsides. Slide in the chops. Raise heat to medium high. This should produce a sizzle and the meat should seize the pan surface. This is what produces attractive, tasty browning. Don't be afraid that you will burn the chops. Just keep your eye on them, and when they have developed a red-brown crust on one side, turn with a spatula and brown the other side the same way.

3. Lower heat to medium and continue to cook until done. Turn thick chops from time to time for even cooking. With lamb, most people prefer pinkish, medium-rare meat once they have tasted it that way. Veal is also at its best when cooked lightly. Pork, on the other hand, should be cooked until it has lost almost all trace of pinkness and is juicy-white right through. Test doneness by cutting into a chop at its thickest point.

4. To make a delicious impromptu sauce, remove the chops to a plate. Pour off most of the fat. Then pour the heavy cream

into the skillet and scrape the pan bottom with a metal spatula to free, or deglaze, the meat juices that have adhered to it. When the cream reaches the boil, pour it through a strainer over the chops.

YIELD: 2 CHOPS

Veal Scallopini

This is a quite expensive cut of meat, but worth it because a small amount of this exquisitely thin and tender veal goes a long way and cooks in a twinkling. This recipe combines the classic procedure for Wiener schnitzel (breaded veal scallopini) with a classic wine sauce. Feel free to eliminate the sauce and substitute lemon wedges on each plate you serve.

> 2 veal scallops
> Salt
> Pepper
> 1 egg, lightly beaten
> ½ cup flour
> ½ cup bread crumbs
> 1 tablespoon butter
> 1 tablespoon oil
> ½ cup white wine or a fortified wine like sherry or the Italian Marsala

1. Veal scallopini, or scallops, should ideally be cut from milk-fed white veal and pounded very thin by the butcher. You can also use mature veal and pound it yourself with a mallet or the side of a cleaver if you don't own the special meat-pounding tool sold for this purpose. The pounding not only produces an elegantly thin and quick-cooking slice of meat but also breaks down the fibers and tenderizes it. These scallops can simply be sautéed quickly in butter, or a mixture of butter and oil (which can be raised to a

higher temperature than butter without burning), in the time it takes to brown them on both sides; or they can be breaded, as follows, and served in an impromptu sauce.

2. Season the scallops with salt and pepper.

3. Dip them in the egg, then the flour, then the bread crumbs. Set them between two sheets of wax paper and press down lightly to make sure that the breading adheres to the meat.

4. Heat the butter and oil together in a skillet and sauté over medium heat until browned on both sides. This happens very quickly; be ready to turn the scallops.

5. Put the scallops on a plate. Then deglaze the skillet by pouring in the white wine or Marsala and scraping the skillet with a metal spatula. When the liquid has boiled briefly, pour it through a strainer over the scallops.

YIELD: 2 VEAL SCALLOPS

Liver and Onions, Venetian Style

In Venice, they long ago discovered that the natural sugar in onions would mask the slight bitterness of liver, and that if liver was cut in strips it would cook quickly and would come out very tender. For this recipe I use beef liver, which is very much cheaper than calf's liver. The flavor is stronger, perhaps, but the onions lighten it.

> ½ pound calf's or beef liver
> Milk
> 1 tablespoon butter
> 1 tablespoon oil
> 1 medium onion, peeled

1. Trim away the membrane from the edge of the liver and discard. Put the liver in a bowl of milk and soak for several hours.

This is an optional step, but it greatly improves the taste and texture of the liver.

2. Heat the butter and oil in a skillet over medium heat.

3. Slice the onion. Separate each slice into its natural rounds and sauté in the skillet until translucent.

4. Meanwhile, drain and slice the liver into ¼-inch-thick strips. Add these to the onions in the skillet and sauté until the liver is cooked through. This happens very quickly. The liver tastes best when it is still lightly pink.

YIELD: 1 SERVING LIVER AND ONIONS

Sautéed Boned Chicken Breasts

Perhaps no other meat dish combines so much elegance, such great speed in preparation and such a low level of cholesterol and calories. The purity of boneless chicken breasts recommends them to the most discriminating palate, but the crystalline refinement of the recipe is achieved with a technique within the grasp of anyone.

1 or 2 boned chicken breasts, cut in half
2 tablespoons butter

1. You can buy breasts already deboned in most supermarket meat departments. It is, however, quite easy and much cheaper to do the boning yourself, just by working carefully with a small, sharp knife. Conventionally, boned breasts are cut in half into 2 delicate pieces, each of which is known as a supreme in French. There are a great many ways of garnishing sautéed chicken breasts. They provided classic chefs with a neutral medium to which they could add almost any sautéed vegetable. You can do the same.

2. Heat the butter in a skillet over medium heat.

3. Slide in the chicken pieces and cook until lightly browned on both sides. This happens very quickly, in 2 or 3 minutes, all

the time it takes to heat through the thin pieces of meat and turn them opaque. The first few times, you will want to test for doneness by cutting into the thickest portion of the supremes or by probing with a trussing needle to make sure that the juices run clear. The danger is that you will turn to some other task and overcook the meat. Dry chicken breasts are failed chicken breasts, stringy and barely edible. Pay attention every minute that you have them in the pan.

YIELD: 1 SERVING CHICKEN BREASTS

Broiled Meat

Like most of the things real men are supposed to be able to do by instinct, broiling thick slabs of red meat actually takes some training and can be brought off brilliantly by women. As a boy, I witnessed my father's self-education at the grill, from those first blackened sirloins to a progressively more refined technique. He built his fires with charcoal, and so did I until I moved into temporary lodgings in the old Gansevoort Market on Manhattan's Lower West Side.

My apartment was perched over a meat warehouse. It had what *The New York Times* real-estate ads called a WBF, a wood-burning fireplace, and a supply of seasoned, split hardwood logs. The meat from my downstairs neighbor was irresistibly inexpensive, but I had to buy it in twenty-pound lots. The result of this microecology was that I broiled steaks constantly over wood. This is surely the best of all methods, but the chanciest, since a wood fire is murder to control and the proper distance of meat from flame is hard to determine and harder to achieve with the normal equipment available in and around a domestic hearth. I jerry-rigged a grill with bricks and a wire shelf from the oven. And, with a bit of practice, I was soon able to produce reliably rare and wood-flavored steaks in my living room. The same spirit of improvisation will help a lot even with manufactured grills and predictable briquettes. It is the rough-and-ready side of broiling—direct heat, decisive judgments about timing and placement and the macho scale of the meat—that has recommended itself traditionally to men. But nothing, as I say, prevents women from indulging the same fantasy of culinary primitivism or from mastering its existential techniques.

Steaks

½ pound beef steak (sirloin or any other cut intended for broiling, especially those sold as London broil)
Salt
Pepper

1. Preheat the broiler.

2. Salt and pepper the meat. Rub in the seasoning. Put the meat on the broiler tray, which should be set as close as possible to the heat without actually bringing the meat in direct contact with it. The idea here is to sear the outside of the meat and warm the interior. This method produces rare or medium-rare steak. If you want your steak well done, don't put it as close to the heat.

3. Leave the broiler (or oven) door open if you can. Broiling should involve direct heat only, not the diffused heat that closing the door will produce. Also, the open door permits casual inspection of the meat. After you see that it has browned nicely on one side, slide the pan out, turn the steak over with a long fork and continue broiling.

4. How long should the meat broil? When is it done? These are unanswerable questions. Thicker meat takes longer than thinner meat. Your rare may not be my rare. A very thin piece may be done as soon as both sides have browned. A 3-inch sirloin could take almost a half hour. Especially when you are new at this, it pays to test the meat by cutting into it at its thickest point. Also, remember that if your steak is thin at one end and thick at the

other, the thin end will cook much faster than the thick one. There is no solution to this dilemma. You are simply going to get some meat rare and some better done, unless you want it all well done, in which case you can throw finesse to the winds, just as long as you don't actually burn the meat.

(I am assuming that you will not want to bother with building a charcoal or wood fire to cook a single steak. But on those occasions when you have a friend or more over for steaks, it will be worthwhile to try outdoor grilling or grilling in a fireplace over a wood fire with a metal grate perched above it. Charcoal and hardwood, especially hardwood, impart a delicious flavor to meat. But it takes at least a half hour for a charcoal or wood fire to settle down into a cooking fire. Each grill or fireplace presents a slightly different logistical problem, as does each fire. It is easy to blacken meat over high flames, but it takes more patience and planning to char the meat lightly and cook its interior. Even professionals have water ready to douse high flames that are encouraged to spring up by dripping meat fat. A baster, a squirt gun or a hose will all let you direct a stream of water and quell the conflagration. A real fire always comes back.)

YIELD: 1 STEAK

Broiled Short Ribs

Every meat counter sells short ribs, but they are a wrongly neglected cut in a nation of steak-and-chop eaters. Koreans, on the other hand, have made short ribs a central event in their highly beef-conscious cuisine. This marinated short-rib preparation is inspired by a clever and tasty standard Korean dish.

   2 short ribs
   Salt
   Pepper

½ cup sesame oil (available at Oriental markets and
health-food stores)

1. Short ribs are a very tasty cut of manageable bulk for a single person (or a couple). They taste even better if you mix together
the salt, pepper and sesame oil in a bowl and marinate the short
ribs in this mixture during the day in the refrigerator. Make sure
you turn the meat about in the marinade so that all sides are coated.
If you can, recoat the meat later in the day (or start the marination
at bedtime and turn the meat in the morning).

2. Drain off excess marinade, if any, and broil as for **steak**
(see previous recipe).

YIELD: 1 SERVING

Shrimp

Many thousands of valuable American man and woman hours have
been spent deveining and shelling shrimp. But if you should happen to observe a Japanese businessman intent on a plate of shrimp
tempura, you will notice that he devours the whole shrimp, which
came to him with its shell on and its sand vein intact underneath
it. He does this not to be bold or because he is too lazy to clean
up what a lazy cook failed to bother with in the first instance. No,
the Japanese eats the shrimp shell because it tastes good; he over-
looks the sand vein because he knows that it is harmless and un-
detectable by the taste buds.

I doubt that I have persuaded you to eat shrimp with their
shells on. But I tried. I don't want to give up, however, without
mentioning that the shells are not only appealingly crunchy but
also tasty, because they pick up the taste of seasonings from the
medium they're cooked in much more readily than the shrimp inside them.

Other than that, there really is very little else to say about basic shrimp cookery except: DON'T OVERCOOK.

Sautéed Shrimp

As with boiled shrimp, these fast-fried ones must not be over-cooked. If they start to curl up, scoop them into a cold serving dish immediately. Also, please do try cooking and eating them with the shells on. This slows down the cooking a tad, and, I'll say it again, the pleasantly crunchy shells pick up the flavor of what they're cooked in. In this case, garlic. You can peel them ahead of time, but don't let me hear about it.

> 2 tablespoons oil
> ½ pound unshelled shrimp
> 2 cloves garlic, minced (see page 43)

1. Sauté the shrimp in very hot oil until heated through, about 5 minutes or less. Add the minced garlic just after you have added the shrimp. Toss the shrimp every few seconds to keep them from burning and to distribute the garlic around them.

YIELD: 1 SERVING

Boiled Shrimp

One hot summer night I observed gluttony at its most basic. My friend Jeffrey, a cook of ambition and refinement, sat down in front of a bowl of these cold boiled shrimp. It was a large bowl with two pounds of unshelled shrimp in it. My plan had been to share this abundance among three of us and have enough left over for my lunch the next day. As it happened, the heat in the air cut my appetite and my other guest's. Jeff methodically ingested a pound and a half of shrimp, leaving a pile of shells. I took this as a compliment, but it was still amazing to watch. If you have a success like this, it will cost you a small fortune. Shrimp are not cheap, but most people find them too rich to eat in real quantity, especially when they are dipped in a real mayonnaise. And when you are by yourself, you can tailor the portion to your appetite and budget.

    ½ **pound shrimp**
    Salt
    Mayonnaise (see page 40)

1. Boil the shrimp in lightly salted water for 5 minutes or until they are heated through. It is almost impossible to underdo shrimp. Remember that overcooked shrimp are rubber; undercooked shrimp are sashimi.

2. Let the shrimp cool and eat with mayonnaise.

YIELD: 1 SERVING

Steamed Lobster

Lobsters should be alive when you buy them, and they will remain alive for a few hours (possibly longer, but who can wait that long to eat them?) in the refrigerator. Capitalizing on this fact, I once liberated a half-dozen lobsters on my kitchen floor at cocktail time, let the heat of the room revive them, and then invited my guests to "catch" their dinner. Drinks had slowed down the guests just enough so that there was some real sport. The lobsters crawled under chairs and showed plenty of gumption. Eventually we had dinner.

This game would not have been possible if lobsters were not naturally portion-controlled. One man (or one woman), one lobster is the rule. Sitting down by one's self to a lobster dinner may sound like an odd form of solitary pleasure, but think about it. It may be a self-indulgence, but what is wrong with a little self-indulgence once in a while?

    1 1½-pound lobster
      Salt
      Melted butter

1. Be sure to refrigerate the lobster until you're ready to cook it. The cold not only keeps *Homarus homarus* fresh but produces lethargy and eliminates lively movements that might make you think better of doing the ugly thing in. No method of killing lobster is entirely appealing. At least I am not asking you to plunge a knife point into the creature's head *à la française*.

2. Plunge the lobster into 1 inch of lightly salted boiling water in a pot large enough to contain the lobster. Cover the pot and steam for 12 minutes. (Should you happen to want to cook more than one lobster, arrange them head down in the pot so that they cook evenly.)

3. Remove the lobster from the pot with a potholder or tongs. As soon as you can, turn it on its back and, using heavy scissors, make an incision the length of the tail and thorax (abdomen). Drain water into the sink. Then lightly crack the shell of the claws with a hammer. Put on a plate and eat with your hands and a small fork and melted butter. The green mass you will eventually encounter is called the tomalley and is entirely edible. In female lobsters there is also a solid red mass called coral, also edible. Do not, however, consume or even pierce a small transparent little bag of evil-tasting matter near the head.

Should anyone ask you, the flat piece at the end of the tail is called the telson.

YIELD: 1 LOBSTER

Sautéed Fish

All fish cook quickly. This makes life easy for the cook, but it also makes it difficult to avoid overcooking fish, because the ideal point of almost firm, incipient flakiness comes and goes so rapidly. For thin pieces of filleted (scaled, gutted, boned and beheaded) fish, timing is everything. But fillets make an ideal meal for a solo dinner. They come in individual portions. So do fish steaks, which are relatively thick slices of largish fish (salmon, swordfish) cut perpendicular to the axis of the vertebra. (Think of a big fish lying on its side. For steaks, you slice along the fish as if it were a long loaf of bread. For fillets, you make an incision down the back of the fish and then work the knife between the flesh and the backbone so as to cut away two long, flattish pieces of flesh running from tail to gills.)

For such small amounts, it makes no sense to think about baking fish, with all the preheating and waiting around that that entails. For a solo meal, the top of the stove is the venue of choice and frying is the method. Although there are literally hundreds of variations on what follows, these two basic methods will work very well indeed for most of the fillets or steaks cut from most of the fish in the world.

Pan-fried Fish

2 tablespoons butter
¼- to ½-pound fish fillet or steak

1. Heat the butter over medium heat. After it melts, foams and then ceases to foam, slide the fish into the pan. Cooking time will vary radically according to the thickness of the piece of fish. With very thin fish such as sole, you should turn it with a spatula after a couple of minutes. A salmon steak will take a little longer.

In any case, take a peek at the underside of the fish and turn it when it has browned lightly.

2. Continue cooking until the fish has cooked through. You can tell this has happened by cutting into the thickest part. The fish is done when the center is opaque. Raw fish is translucent or at least shiny. It turns opaque and a bit duller when heated.

You can speed along the cooking of a very thick fish steak by putting a lid on the pan. Check on the fish's progress frequently.

YIELD: 1 SERVING

Fried Breaded Fish

This is an unattractive but accurate way of naming one of the planet's most universally favored methods of preparing fish. There is not much difference between this method and plain frying. Here you just pour some cornmeal on a plate and press the fish in it on all sides. The natural moisture of the fish will make the cornmeal cling to it. Shake off the excess and fry as in previous recipe.

Eggs

Omelet

This is a recipe for a plain omelet. You can fill it with almost anything, from diced fried potatoes to grated Swiss cheese to asparagus tips cooked in advance and dropped onto the omelet just before it gets folded up. To make an *omelette aux fines herbes,* the classic French dish flavored with chopped herbs such as parsley, chives or tarragon, mix a tablespoonful or so of the herbs into the eggs as you beat them.

> 2 **eggs**
> **Salt**
> **Pepper**
> 1 **tablespoon butter**
> ¼ **chopped parsley (see page 43)**

1. Crack the eggs into a bowl and beat them lightly with a fork. Beat only until the whites and yolks have merged, and as you beat add the salt and pepper.

2. Heat the butter over high heat in a 7-inch omelet pan (or at least a small skillet with a very smooth surface. Nonstick synthetic surfaces are excellent. The omelet must slide like a skate on ice). When the foam subsides, pour the egg mixture into the pan and count to three slowly. Then shake the pan vigorously at a slight angle to the burner (handle up), once per second until the egg mass thickens slightly, as it slides back and forth against the far side of the pan. This will happen quite rapidly. (You should add any filling at this point, about ¼ cup.)

3. Do not hesitate. Raise the handle and shake it so that the omelet rolls forward into a neat package. Hold over heat another second to brown the bottom. Then roll out onto a plate.

It is possible to make larger omelets with more eggs for more people. But the best and easiest procedure is to cook individual omelets, one at a time for each guest. You have much more control this way and are much more likely to end up with omelets that are soft and moist inside, as they should be.

YIELD: 1 OMELET

Vegetables

This is only a small selection of vegetables, those whose preparation particularly suits a single diner. Look for other vegetable recipes, which can be cut down in quantity quite easily, in Chapters 6–8.

Artichoke

This sounds like more work than it actually is. The real work is in the eating of this edible thistle, which in this country almost inevitably comes from Castroville, California, near Monterey. There is a restaurant there shaped like an artichoke next to fields almost surrealistically full of artichoke plants.

> 1 **artichoke**
> ½ **lemon**
> 12 **black peppercorns**
> **Salt**
> **Melted butter** *or* **vinaigrette dressing** (see page 53)

1. Boil enough water to cover the artichoke comfortably. Test this by holding the artichoke in the water before you start heating it.

2. Snap off the stem of the artichoke; this pulls out unwanted fibers along with it. Then cut a slice off the bottom of the artichoke to flatten it so that it will sit straight on a plate. Rub the bottom with the lemon to prevent its turning black from contact with the air.

3. Pull off the tiny leaves at the base of the artichoke. Lay the artichoke on its side and slice off about two inches from the top, thereby removing unwanted pointy leaf tips and creating a flat top.

Rub all cut surfaces with the lemon. Then take scissors and trim away all remaining leaf tips. Rub cut places with lemon.

4. Put the lemon, peppercorns and salt into the boiling water. Then put in the artichoke, bottom down. It will float. To keep it submerged, rest a small skillet over it. If that isn't heavy enough, weight the skillet. Boil for approximately 30 minutes. If the artichoke is small, test by probing the bottom with a fork after 20 minutes. If the fork goes in with fair ease, the artichoke is done.

5. Drain the artichoke by letting it rest upside down in the sink. It will stay hot for much longer than it takes to drain. In fact, if you intend to eat the artichoke within ½ hour of cooking it, it will be hot and should be accompanied by melted butter. Cold artichokes are served with vinaigrette.

YIELD: 1 ARTICHOKE

Asparagus

To plant asparagus in a garden is an act of faith in the future. The first harvestable crop won't come in for three years. I have now survived the waiting period and in June I can have as many fresh asparagus as I want. There are some young shoots so thin and tender that I eat them raw in the garden. They cook in an instant. Thicker stalks obviously take longer. Advocates of the crunchy vegetable immerse their asparagus in boiling water, turn off the heat and wait one minute before removing the asparagus. If you are not sure what you like in terms of texture or what will achieve it, test one stalk, nibbling at the bottom after a couple of minutes and putting it back for more cooking if you don't like the results the first time around. Then do the whole batch.

½ **pound asparagus**
  Salt
2 **tablespoons butter, melted**

1. With a sharp small knife, pare away the tough outer layer at the butt end of each asparagus. If you don't do this, you will end up not eating the butt ends because they will be too woody to chew. You should be able to tell how much to cut away—up to ⅟₁₆ inch at the bottom and less and less as the stalk gets more tender toward the top. Stop cutting when you reach the green part.

2. Bring a large quantity of lightly salted (1½ teaspoons salt per quart) water to a boil in a pot large enough to hold the asparagus laid horizontally.

3. While the water comes to a boil, tie the asparagus into a bundle with two lengths of string. Tie one just below the tips and the other a couple of inches from the butt ends. Line the asparagus up at their tips. After you've tied the bundle, cut just enough off the ends to even them up.

4. Put the asparagus into the water. After the water returns to the boil, reduce heat and simmer for 2 to 10 minutes or until a knife pierces the butt end of the thickest stalk easily. You can maneuver the bundle by catching on to one of the strings with a fork.

5. Drain the asparagus. Then set in a serving platter or directly on a plate. Cut strings and discard. Pour melted butter over the asparagus. Or serve cold with **vinaigrette** (see page 53).

YIELD: 1 SERVING

Baked Potato

Restaurants tend to prepare baked potatoes badly. They bake them in advance, at least partially, and let them sit around. At home, you can easily time this almost labor-free delicacy to perfection. It should be cooked through evenly, with no layer of dried out crust just inside the jacket. The ideal taste, to my mind, comes from the counterpoint between smoothness and starchiness that a true baking potato allows. Let no one tell you that a baked potato is a plebeian food. Centuries of connoisseurship in its native Peru and later in Europe have developed our modern varieties. They are the result of loving horticulture and should be venerated as such.

1 large baking (Idaho) potato
1 pat butter

1. Preheat oven to 425 degrees. For a single potato, you and the energy shortage are better off if you use a toaster oven.
2. Set the potato directly on a rack in the oven or toaster oven.
3. Bake for 45 minutes or until a fork or trussing needle goes into the potato easily.
4. Split the potato with a knife. Put on a plate and place the pat of butter on top to melt.

YIELD: 1 BAKED POTATO

Desserts

When you're by yourself, you should not spend time fussing with dessert cookery. Few made desserts are really meant just for one person. Eat fruit and cheese. Bake pies and cakes for company.

6

TABLES
FOR TWO

FOR TWO PEOPLE WHO ARE HAPPY TO BE ALONE WITH EACH other, almost any menu will be a success. But the most appropriate dishes for couples to serve themselves are those foods they wouldn't want to serve gangs of outsiders. What do I mean? Basically two categories of recipes: the unwieldy and the unusual. Dishes that take a lot of hand work are dishes you wouldn't want to tackle for a party of fourteen. Ditto for bulky foods that crowd the oven or the stove top. And then there are "special" ingredients, for example unpopular but delicious cuts of meat, especially organ meats you would only risk on yourself and on others you know well enough to be sure they like the same oddments you do.

In terms of quantity, any of the dishes in the previous chapter can be doubled and served for two instead of one. But the recipes in this chapter are ideally suited for couples who cook. After you've made these dishes and eaten them a few times, you will see why they work out so well on the practical level for two people, and then, after you've come to connect them with intimate dining, they will take on a private luster. You could double most of them, or even triple them without a ridiculously excessive outlay of effort, but you may find that these are food experiences you won't want to share with just anyone.

Moules Marinière
(Mussels Steamed in White Wine)

Mussels are one of America's great untapped resources. These delicious, inexpensive shellfish abound on both coasts. They cook in seconds. And some markets have begun to eliminate their sole traditional drawback. In the old days, you had to clean them with a wire brush, because they had been plucked off of the primal sea floor and only lightly rinsed. These days, mussels are more and more the product of an organized farming program. And when they are seeded on boards or bricks just above the sea bottom, they grow up cleaner—and fatter. This is not yet true of all mussels, and even the clean ones have to have their fuzzy little beards pulled; so there is work to be done, and it is the kind of work that increases in a straight line as you try to serve more mussels to more people. You'll barely notice the job, however, if you save this treat for just the two of you.

2 quarts fresh mussels, in the shell
1 small onion, chopped (see page 39)
5 parsley stems
1 bay leaf
¼ teaspoon dried thyme
2 ribs celery, trimmed and chopped
Pepper
3 tablespoons butter
1 cup dry white wine

1. If the mussels are not clean—shiny and black—scrub them with a steel brush or steel wool. Pull away the beard that dangles from between the two shells of most of the mussels and discard. Discard any mussels that are open or either noticeably heavier or lighter than normal. Soak the rest in cold water for 2 hours. THIS STEP IS ESSENTIAL. The soaking purges the grit that makes mussels inedible.

2. In a 4- to 5-quart pot (ideally, a pot you can serve from at the table), combine all ingredients except mussels. Bring to a boil, uncovered, and cook three minutes.

3. Add mussels and cook for 5 minutes over medium-high heat. After 3 minutes, stir the mussels with a large wooden spoon. The mussels are done when they have opened. Serve immediately, spooning out a pile of mussels into each of two large soup bowls. Ladle the cooking liquid over them. Eat with hands and whatever other implement seems right.

YIELD: 2 SERVINGS

Grilled Breast of Lamb

This tasty, cheap cut is often passed by because of the numerous bones that transsect it. Here is a recipe that shows the French genius for transforming a humble ingredient into an elegant but thrifty showpiece. You parcook the meat ahead of time, to the point where the bones can be pulled out easily and discarded. Then you flatten it so that it can be treated as if it were a luxurious piece of veal scallopini. Then, the next day, you bread and grill it—brilliance in a trice.

2 tablespoons butter
1 medium onion, chopped (see page 39)
3 carrots, peeled and cut into rounds
1 pound lamb breast
  Flour
2 eggs
  Salt
  Pepper
  Bread crumbs
4 tablespoons butter, melted

1. Melt the butter over medium heat in a skillet, and when the foam has subsided, add the onion and carrots and sauté until the onion is translucent.

2. Transfer the onion-carrot mixture to a pot or a pan large enough to contain the lamb breast. Add the lamb and just enough water to cover the meat. Bring the liquid to a boil; then reduce heat until you produce a very slow simmer.

3. Continue cooking until the bones in the lamb have loosened, about an hour. Test with tongs. When you succeed in loosening a bone, remove the meat, drain and extract the rest of the bones immediately, while the meat is still hot. Save the cooking liquid for a soup.

4. Spread the meat on half of a clean dish towel. Fold the other half of the towel over the meat. Put a cutting board that is at least as large as the meat on top of the towel. Then place a weight of about 10 pounds on top of the board. Let stand for 2 hours.

5. Take out the flattened meat and cut it into uniform triangles with sides of about 2 inches.

6. Preheat the broiler.

7. Set up a small assembly line for breading the lamb triangles *à l'anglaise,* in the English style. In a plate or a bowl, put ½ cup of flour, more or less. Crack the eggs into a bowl and beat them lightly, until the whites and yolks have merged. Season with salt and pepper as you beat. Last, put a handful of bread crumbs on a plate.

8. Spear a lamb triangle with a fork. Dip it in the flour to coat it lightly. This dries the surface of the meat and allows it to take up the egg more uniformly. Now dip the lamb piece in the egg. Then move it to the bread crumbs and dredge it (drag it back and forth in the bread crumbs) so as to coat the surface completely. Set the triangle on the greased rack or pan you will use later to run it under the broiler. Continue breading the lamb in this manner until you have finished with all the triangles. Try to time the breading so that you can move ahead to broiling quite soon. If you wait a long time, the breading will dry out.

9. Drizzle the lamb pieces with melted butter. Set the rack or

pan at the lowest position in the broiler. Keep an eye on things right along, as your goal is only a light browning of the surface of the triangles. When they have browned on one side, turn them over, drizzle with butter again and brown the other side. When browned, they should also be heated through and ready to serve.

YIELD: 2 SERVINGS

Pasta

Pasta is great for crowds. Some versions of pasta. Others are virtuoso productions you wouldn't think of trying for more than four. For two, they are even easier on the cook. If you memorize the basic method of boiling pasta, you will be able to apply it to almost all the hundreds of shapes and sizes that are manufactured. Then you can improvise sauces from ingredients already at hand: Just sauté chopped garlic in ½ cup of olive oil and pour over the cooked pasta; sauté a mixture of sliced or chopped fresh vegetables; or cobble together your own version of *spaghetti bolognese,* with sautéed chopped meat and chopped fresh or canned Italian tomatoes. The sauces spelled out below are glamorous classics, just a touch elaborate—in the number of their ingredients, not their technique—but worth the few extra stops in the market.

Spaghetti alla Carbonara

This is a classic pasta of Rome, noodles tossed in egg and garnished with bits of bacon. The name derives from the Italian word for coal, *carbone.* When you grind the black pepper over this elegant dish, it will resemble a cloud of coal dust.

1 tablespoon olive oil
1 small onion, chopped (see page 39)
¼ pound bacon (buy unsmoked bacon, called *pancetta,* at an Italian deli if you possibly can, for the authentic taste)
¼ cup dry white wine
½ pound spaghetti
Salt
1 egg yolk
3 tablespoons heavy cream
¼ cup freshly grated Romano cheese
Freshly ground black pepper

1. Heat the oil in a small skillet and sauté the onion and bacon (see page 108) until the onion is translucent. If you are using American-style bacon, it should be cut into 1-inch strips. Dice *pancetta.*

2. Add wine, lower heat until wine just bubbles. Cook another 10 minutes. By then, the wine should have evaporated and the bacon should be cooked but not crisped.

3. Meanwhile, bring 4 quarts of lightly salted water to a full rolling boil in a 6-quart pot. The salt is not an affectation; the pasta will not taste as good without it. Drop in the pasta all at once and cook for about 10 minutes. After 8 minutes, taste a strand. It is done when it is cooked through but still slightly chewy. Italians call this condition *al dente:* The noodles cling to the tooth.

4. While the pasta is boiling, beat the egg yolk with the heavy cream in a bowl until they are well blended.

5. Drain the spaghetti by dumping it along with its cooking water into a colander securely placed in the sink. Be careful. You should expect a surprisingly powerful gust of scalding steam to burst upward as you upend the pot. When the water has drained out of the colander, dump the spaghetti into a capacious serving bowl.

6. Mix in the egg-cream mixture. Work in a little at a time, stirring vigorously after each addition so that the egg does not scramble. Then stir in the Romano cheese.

7. Add the bacon or *pancetta* mixture. And, finally, grind pepper over the bowl and serve immediately.

YIELD: 2 SERVINGS

Spaghetti alla Puttanesca

Literally, this is whore-style spaghetti. But what does that mean? Are the *puttane* of the Via Appia Antica outside Rome excellent cooks who attract customers with food? That is one etymology for *puttanesca* I have heard. Another, more persuasive, is that exhausted hookers throw together this spicy and aromatic dish as a pick-me-up at the end of their work hours. Respectable people also can and do enjoy this intrinsically racy dish. The only hard part is assembling all the ingredients in one place before you start. Don't worry if you don't have every single one of them, however, since there is no hard-and-fast recipe for *puttanesca*.

> 3 tablespoons olive oil
> 3 cloves garlic, finely chopped (see page 43)
> 3 anchovy fillets, roughly chopped
> 2 peeled Italian tomatoes, drained (optional)
> 1 tablespoon capers
> ¼ cup pitted Italian or Greek black olives
> 3 ounces canned tuna
> 1 dried red chili, crumbled (or red pepper flakes), to taste
> 1 teaspoon chopped parsley (see page 43)
> 1 basil leaf, torn into little pieces, *or* 1 pinch dried basil
> Pepper
> Salt
> ½ pound spaghetti

1. Heat the olive oil in a skillet. Over medium-high heat, cook the garlic for a moment, to release flavor. Then add anchovies and

mash together with the garlic. After a couple of minutes, add the tomatoes, if you're going to (this addition is becoming standard, but I think the dish is purer in its brio without them), and cook slowly for 15 minutes.

2. Add capers, olives, tuna, chili, parsley, basil and pepper. Stir the mixture as it heats through and try to mash it into a paste. Set aside.

3. Bring 4 quarts of lightly salted water to a boil and cook spaghetti as in previous recipe.

4. Toss the spaghetti with the sauce in a serving bowl. Serve immediately.

YIELD: 2 SERVINGS

Spareribs

Barbecued Spareribs

There are as many barbecue sauces as there are people who barbecue. The great majority include ketchup or chili sauce. Do not hesitate to stir ½ cup or more into the marinade below.

    4 pounds spareribs
    1 cup oil
    ½ cup vinegar
    ½ cup soy sauce
    3 cloves garlic, finely chopped
    1 teaspoon whole black peppercorns
    ½ teaspoon Cayenne pepper

1. Put the ribs in a pan that will hold them laid flat in a single layer.

2. In a bowl, mix all other ingredients and pour the resulting

marinade over the ribs. Turn the ribs so that they are completely covered. Refrigerate for 24 hours. Turn the ribs from time to time during this period.

3. Build a wood or charcoal fire for cooking. Or preheat the oven to 350 degrees.

4. If you are cooking over an open fire, set the metal rack about 4 inches from the heat (or, if the rack is not conveniently adjustable, arrange the fire so that it is 4 inches from the rack) and lay down the ribs. You should try to cook over a fire that is hot, but not an inferno of licking flames. Dripping fat will soon cause a conflagration, which you must be prepared to quell with water from a pitcher, squirt gun or baster. Turn the ribs frequently. Baste with the marinade left in the pan. They should be done—brown and cooked through—in about 1¼ hours, if not sooner.

Follow the same overall routine if cooking ribs in the oven. Cooking time will be about 1½ hours.

YIELD: 2 SERVINGS

Spareribs with Garlic Sauce

I once wandered into a nondescript tavern in central Frankfurt, West Germany, and saw a romantic couple eating something that smelled wonderful with a single fork and knife. I asked the waitress what it was and she replied *"Leiterchen mit Knoblauchsosse"* (a little ladder with garlic sauce).

I ordered it and found out that "ladderlet" was the colorful and quite accurate Frankfurt dialectal way of naming a rack of ribs. It was delicious, and came with a green bean and onion salad, potatoes and local hard cider.

    4 pounds spareribs
    2 tablespoons pureed garlic (see page 43)

1. Preheat oven to 350 degrees.

2. Lay the spareribs down in a pan in a single layer. Spread them on both sides with the garlic puree.

3. Bake for 1½ hours or until the ribs are browned and cooked through. Turn every 15 minutes.

YIELD: 2 SERVINGS

Poultry

Frie*d* Chicken

Great fortunes have been made purveying this classic Southern food idea to millions of hungry people in other regions. It is the most successful of all traditional American regional dishes. But even, or perhaps especially, as a fast food, fried chicken is a quite variable recipe. Some like it crisp; others like it seasoned sharply. There are fast chicken chains for every taste. But I think none of them matches the quality of chicken fried at home. It is almost as convenient to do it yourself—and a lot cheaper—than waiting in the plastic glare of a fast-food place and letting Colonel Whoever-he-is decide how much "secret" spice mixture to use.

This recipe is meant only as a basic guideline. Once you have tried it, you will certainly want to fiddle with the spicing. If you like hot food, you may want to join the vocal subculture that adds plenty of Cayenne pepper to the basic flour mixture.

The quantity of chicken called for here is a deliberately generous amount for two people with normal appetites. But, as you have already observed, some people eat piles of chicken, even when it isn't very good. Should there be any of your impeccable fried chicken left over, it will be just fine served cold the next day.

(Traditional Southern cooks use lard for frying, because that was the fat their forebears had in abundance. I prefer it today, because it adds personality to the flavor of the chicken.)

2½ pounds chicken, cut into serving pieces
1 cup flour
½ teaspoon salt
¼ teaspoon black pepper
Lard or oil for frying

1. Chill the chicken (if it has been in the refrigerator overnight or more, leave it there until you are ready to cook it).

2. In a bowl, sift or mix together the flour, salt and pepper. Pour the mixture in a paper bag large enough to hold all the chicken pieces.

3. Take a skillet (or skillets) large enough to hold the chicken. Fill it (them) to a depth of ½ inch with the lard (melt it a bit at a time over low heat until you have the right amount) or oil. Use medium-high heat. You want the lard or oil to be quite hot but not smoking when you put the chicken into it. If it starts to smoke, reduce heat a bit but not drastically.

4. While lard or oil is heating, put chicken in the paper bag and shake gently to cover the pieces thoroughly. This method is quick, efficient and allows you to keep your hands off the chicken, leaving the flour where it should be, not on your fingers.

5. Put the bag on the stove top near the skillet. Tear it open. Disturbing the flour as little as possible (picking the chicken up with tongs or a serving fork), put the chicken into the skillet(s). Cover (to promote even cooking) and cook for about 6 minutes or until the pieces have browned underneath. You may have to adjust the heat to maintain a good bubble in the lard or oil after the chicken has been put in and lowers the temperature. This is not a violent process, but you will have to peek after a couple of minutes to make sure there is no smoke or burning.

Turn, cover again and continue cooking for another 6 minutes or until the other sides are browned and the thickest part of a thigh or leg is cooked. The juices should run clear when pricked with a fork.

6. Drain on paper toweling.

YIELD: 2 SERVINGS

Roast Duck

Even though they are fully domesticated and full of fat (which has to be almost completely eliminated in cooking), ducks retain some of their ancestral nature as wild birds. They are not gamy, but they are all dark meat and should be cooked so that the breast meat is medium rare. Modern French cooks treat the breasts like steak, which they resemble very closely in certain preparations. Roast duck is a perfect dish for a special dinner for two. Neither diner has to perform suicidal feats of valor in the kitchen. There will be no leftovers.

1 3-pound duck

1. Preheat oven to 325 degrees.
2. Put duck, breast up, on a rack in a roasting pan. Set pan on a rack in the middle of the oven.
3. After 20 minutes, turn the duck over. Prick the back and sides to let the fat drip out.
4. Continue cooking until the bird is done. Duck should be served medium rare. Juices will run light pink. Allow about 25 minutes per pound, calculating from the start of roasting. Do not baste. But remove fat from the roasting pan with a baster or a large serving spoon from time to time during roasting. I save duck fat and use it for frying potatoes. Not everyone likes it, and some authorities advise discarding it. Try it and see.

YIELD: 2 GENEROUS SERVINGS

Broiled Quail

Frozen quails of high quality have begun to appear widely in supermarkets. Like most game animals, quails do not suffer from freezing. But unlike deer and pheasant, they thrive when raised on farms, and their flesh retains its "wild" personality. They are small but toothsome little birds, too small, in fact, to be eaten profitably with knife and fork. Use your hands.

My wife invented this recipe, building on two standard notions: The first was that game benefits in taste and tenderness from an immersion in a marinade, which is fundamentally a seasoned oil and vinegar (**vinaigrette**) salad dressing (see basic recipe, page 53). The second was that a sauce sweetened with fruit or fruit jelly makes a fine match with the strong taste of game. Quails are so refined to begin with that these measures are not strictly necessary, as they would be with, say, bear haunch. But they definitely enhance the taste of the quail, and they add just the right hint of the hunt, by purely gastronomic means of great simplicity. In other words, the marination and the dollop of currant jelly make an unmistakable allusion to other game recipes.

> 4 quails
> ½ cup olive oil
> 1 tablespoon vinegar
>   Salt
>   Pepper
> 2 tablespoons red currant jelly

1. Marinate quails in a salad dressing stirred together from the oil, vinegar, salt and pepper for 2 hours at room temperature, turning occasionally.

2. Preheat broiler.

3. Set the quails in a roasting pan, and place 6 or 7 inches from the broiler flame or element.

4. Turn the birds every 5 minutes or so, and baste them with the marinating liquid.

5. After 15 minutes, swirl the currant jelly into the pan juices. Using tongs, dip the birds into the jelly-pan juice mixture so as to coat them all over.

6. Test the birds for doneness. They are ready to eat when the outsides are browned and the juices from the breast run clear if you prick the birds with a fork. Serve immediately.

YIELD: 2 SERVINGS

Innards

Sautéed Veal Kidneys

A butcher you trust will sell fresh kidneys. They will not have the strong, acrid flavor that has given kidneys a bad name in some quarters.

The rest depends on you. Swift cooking at very high heat will prevent the kidneys from releasing their juices, boiling in them and toughening up.

> 1 **veal kidney (about ½ pound)**
> 1 **tablespoon butter**
> 1 **tablespoon oil**
> 1 **teaspoon flour**
> ½ **cup Madeira or white wine**
>   **Salt**
>   **Pepper**

1. Cut the kidney in half, lengthwise, so as to expose the lingering pieces of white fat in the interior. Cut away the fat and discard.

2. Slice the kidney into rounds about ¼-inch thick.

3. In a small, heavy skillet, heat the butter and oil until they smoke. Then, right away, dump in the kidney slices and spread them out in the pan. In 2 or 3 minutes they will turn gray. Turn them with a spatula while they cook. A certain amount of pink at the center is desirable. Do not attempt to brown them. This will release the juices and ruin everything.

4. Sprinkle the kidneys with the flour. Stir them quickly and add the wine, salt and pepper. This stops the cooking. Let the wine heat up but do not permit it to boil. Serve immediately.

YIELD: 2 SERVINGS

Calf's Brains in Brown Butter

This is a delicate, rich standby of French homecooking. The French name for brown butter is *beurre noir,* literally black butter. But the color you want to strive for is a nutty brown (the taste is nutlike also), produced by heating the butter until usually invisible milk solids in it are browned in the hot butterfat. Vinegar adds an attractive sour tang to the butter. This is a sauce that comes in two parts. You can't pour the vinegar directly into the hot butter because it would react violently.

Brains, like sweetbreads, require somewhat lengthy soaking (to remove their outer membranes and the exterior blood). This is a task you will cease to mind almost as soon as you plunge in, and especially after you have learned to appreciate the elegance of brains.

   ½ **pound calf's brains**
   6 **tablespoons vinegar**
   1 **teaspoon salt**

Pepper
1 clove garlic, peeled (see page 43)
1 bay leaf
¼ teaspoon dried thyme
6 tablespoons butter

1. Soak the brains in 3 quarts of cold water for 2 hours. Remove the brains carefully from the water with a slotted spoon. Pull away the outer membrane. It should peel away quite easily. Then soak the brains in 3 quarts of fresh water acidulated with 3 tablespoons of vinegar for another 2 hours. This will loosen the blood. Drain the brains and trim away the solid white pieces at the bases.

2. In a nonaluminum saucepan, cover the brains with cold water. Add 1 tablespoon of vinegar, the salt, pepper, garlic, bay leaf and thyme. Bring to a boil and immediately reduce heat so that the water just trembles. Poach, uncovered, for 20 minutes.

3. Remove the brains from the water with a slotted spoon. Drain completely and set on a serving platter.

4. Melt the butter in a small skillet and cook over medium-high heat until it turns a nutty brown. As soon as this happens, which will be very quickly, pour over the brains. Then, without delay, heat the remaining 2 tablespoons of vinegar in the skillet. Reduce to half its original volume at a brisk boil. This will also be a matter of moments. Pour over brains and serve.

YIELD: 2 SERVINGS

Vegetables

Peas

You can get by nicely enough, I suppose, with frozen peas (but let's agree that canned peas are repulsive and fit only for survival cooking during a nuclear winter). And yet fresh peas really are worth the bother of shelling from their pods. They are sweet, and they are not all the same size.

When you are buying (or picking) peas in the pod, figure that 1 pound of them will yield roughly ¼ pound of peas. This is just about the standard amount for two people, but it might strike you as being on the skimpy side because you are going to like these peas so much. So let's say that 1¼ pounds of unshelled peas will be the judicious amount to get for two people. In the garden, where you probably don't want to bring a scale, you could bring a measuring cup and measure out 5 cups of unshelled peas.

Salt
1¼ pounds (5 cups) unshelled peas
Butter

1. Bring 4 quarts of lightly salted water to a full rolling boil in a large pot. Meanwhile, shell the peas: Press each pod between thumb and forefinger until it pops open; collect the string of green peas in a bowl and discard the pods.

2. Dump the shelled peas all at once into the boiling water. The reason you are using such a large quantity of water is to make sure that the addition of the peas does not significantly lower the water temperature below the boiling point. You don't want the peas to sit around getting soggy in tepid water. You want them to cook at a full boil. This principle holds for all vegetables cooked in boiling water.

3. Boil for 5 minutes. Drain in a colander and dump into a

big skillet. Set over low heat to dry the surfaces of the peas completely. This is to make sure that when you add butter, moisture remaining on the surface of the peas does not keep the butter from sticking to them, instead making it run off and collect in a pool at the bottom of the bowl. The drying should take place in a trice: Shake the pan to move the peas around and expose them all to the heat. Then remove the skillet from the heat. Add butter in small pieces and sprinkle with salt. The combined heat of the pan and the peas themselves will melt the butter, but to encourage this and to spread the butter around (without endangering the perfection of the peas with damage from a spoon or fork), slide the skillet in a circle on the counter for 1 or 2 minutes.

YIELD: 2 SERVINGS

Green Beans

Fresh young green beans are a horse of an entirely different color from frozen beans (I don't need to tell you about horrible canned green beans). When fresh beans appear in vegetable and farmers' markets, you are presented with one of the strongest arguments for cooking at home. Actually, with green beans, as with painting a wall, it is the preparation that takes a bit of doing. The cooking, like the painting, is quick and easy. Trimming green beans is, however, one of those simple, repetitive tasks for which others can be enlisted. Nothing prevents you from having a glass of wine and a conversation while you work together.

> 1 pound fresh green beans
> Salt
> Butter

1. Cut the tips off both ends of all the beans. Wash in cold water. Sort them by width. It should be sufficient to create three

piles, one for the thinnest, one for the thickest and one for the ones midway between.

2. Bring 6 quarts of lightly salted water to the boil.

3. Plunge the thickest beans into the water. Wait 2 minutes and add the medium pile. Wait another 2 minutes and add the rest of the beans. Continue cooking for approximately 10 more minutes. Do not cover the pot. The beans are done when they have softened and turned a lively green, but not turned limp. They should present some resistance to the tooth.

The large amount of water allows you to add the cold beans without overwhelming the temperature. A full boil should resume almost immediately. Sorting the beans helps to ensure that they all come out properly done at the same time.

4. Drain in a colander. Then dump the beans into a skillet and dry out over low heat for 2 or 3 minutes, shaking the pan to flip the beans. Remove from heat and transfer to a serving dish. Cut bits of butter into the beans. Cover to speed melting of the butter. Serve immediately. Any leftovers can be served cold with **vinaigrette dressing** (see page 53) as a salad or a summer vegetable course.

YIELD: 2 SERVINGS

Beets

Fresh beets are a miracle of flavor and ease of preparation. They are really two vegetables in one. The red beets come with green leafy tops. These should be washed thoroughly and steamed like spinach (see page 204). The beets themselves go right into boiling water and are peeled after cooking, at which point they can be sliced and served hot; or diced, marinated briefly in **vinaigrette dressing** (see page 53) and served with endive in a salad; or mixed with **mayonnaise** (see page 40) seasoned heavily with chopped garlic (see page 43).

1¾ pounds beets, weighed with leaves
Salt
Butter

1. Bring 4 quarts of water to the boil.

2. Meanwhile, cut off the leafy tops and refrigerate for future use (see above). Rinse the beets.

3. Put the beets in the boiling water. Add a tablespoon of salt. Reduce heat until the water just simmers. Continue cooking, uncovered, until a fork easily goes into the largest beet. This will take varying amounts of time, but count on ½ hour on the average.

4. Drain the beets and set on a Formica counter (the juices will stain wood) or on newspaper. As soon as they are cool enough to handle, rub off the outer skin, which will peel away readily. The root and the remnant of the top will also pull away easily. If you are rushed, you could do this job without waiting for the beets to cool by spearing them with a fork and protecting your hand with a rubber glove.

5. Slice the beets thinly. Put the slices in a serving dish and cut butter onto them. The heat of the beets will melt the butter.

YIELD: 2 SERVINGS

French-fried Vegetables

There are many ways to skin this particular cat. But all roads lead to the same Rome: crisp slivers or rounds fried rapidly in a bath of very hot oil. Thermostated deep fryers eliminate a bit of guesswork about temperature. So do deep-frying thermometers (candy thermometers cover the same range of heat and will suffice for this job). In what follows, however, I am trying, as usual, to dispense with gadgetry and to encourage rugged simplicity and the awakening of good cooking instincts through the application of low-tech methods, modest equipment and common sense.

What you need, at a minimum, for deep frying, is a saucepan and a device for removing the fried food when it is cooked. Assuming you already have a saucepan, you should acquire either a skimmer (a senior version of the slotted spoon called an *écumoire* in French equipment stores) or a wire-mesh fry basket with a handle on it. The fry basket nests in an average saucepan. You put the food in it, lower everything into the hot oil, leave it there until the frying is done and then lift it out carefully and let the food drain right in it.

If you don't have a thermostat or a thermometer, what do you do? Wait for the oil to smoke is what you do. But don't wait any longer or the oil will degenerate into an unusable, dark, burned mess and leave a greasy deposit from its vapors all over everything. But if you put the food in right away, this lowers the temperature of the oil to a point where all goes well. If you notice smoke after cooking begins, lower the heat a bit and/or remove the pan from the burner altogether for quick relief; then return it after the heat is reduced. If you think the food is cooking too fast on the outside—a sign of excessive heat—lower heat slightly for the next batch. This may sound dreadfully empirical, but once you work it out—for your stove and your saucepan and its quantity of oil—you can just fry away like any teenage fry chef at McDonald's. In practice, it is rare to overdo the temperature of the oil through simple blundering. Mistakes tend to occur in the other direction: Food plopped into oil not hot enough soaks up the oil and emerges sodden and dreadful.

You can achieve slightly better precision about temperature by testing the oil with pieces of bread crust (see following recipe). If you are careful and don't leave the oil to burn after you're done frying, you can strain it—AFTER IT HAS COOLED, bottle it and reuse it, more than once.

Be careful. Deep frying takes place in a temperature range somewhere between 350 and 400 degrees Fahrenheit. This is hot stuff. Don't touch it, and don't spill it on yourself. Also, cook food in small batches. This is essential for cooking at high temperature and it eliminates the risk of overflowing oil. When you put cold food in hot oil, you produce a small explosion of vaporizing water. Too much food means a Vesuvius of steam and a dangerous and wasteful little eruption all over the place.

French-fried Potatoes

2 large Maine potatoes
Oil
Salt

1. Peel the potatoes. Use a vegetable peeler, working your way around the potato until it is all peeled. Cut away the eyes, the little pockmarks on the surface of the potato, but only if they are large enough to bother you.

2. Cut the potatoes lengthwise into sticks. Do this by first halving the potato, then halving the halves and so on until you are left with potato sticks somewhat thinner than ½ inch. The actual thickness is up to you, but the thinner they are the crisper they get and the less starch there will be at the center.

Wrap the cut potatoes in a dish towel to keep them from browning in contact with air while they wait to be cooked.

3. Fill a 3-quart saucepan halfway with oil. Set over high heat, uncovered, and wait, either until the oil just begins to smoke or until it registers 370 on a frying thermometer. If you have no thermometer and want to estimate 370 degrees, drop a piece of bread crust into the oil from time to time. As soon as the oil takes notice of the crust by shaking or bubbling slightly, it has reached about 370. If you wait for the oil to smoke, it will be a touch high for ideal frying, but it will work anyway. Whatever method you use to estimate oil temperature, when the moment arrives, gently lower a handful of potato sticks (but not with your hand; use a skimmer or a fry basket).

4. Cook 7 minutes. Remove the potatoes in the fry basket or with a skimmer. Let excess oil drain back into the pan and then dump the potatoes onto paper toweling. Continue cooking the potatoes in this manner until they are all used up. The potatoes are essentially cooked now, but they go back into the oil another time, just before serving, for a final crisping session at higher heat. In between, they can wait about an hour without suffering.

5. The oil temperature should ideally be at 380 for this stage. Bread crusts dropped in 380-degree oil will make the oil foam up vigorously. Take a cup or so of the parcooked potato sticks and immerse in the oil for 1 or 2 minutes. They will take on a golden-brown color. Remove and drain on paper toweling. Continue cooking until all the potatoes are finished. Sprinkle with salt and serve. If you have to hold the finished potatoes any length of time, keep them, uncovered, in a low (225-degree) oven.

YIELD: 2 SERVINGS

French-fried Zucchini

Zucchini are universally available in the United States at all times of the year. They are not normally an inspiring vegetable, especially the giant tasteless monsters that home gardeners bring when they come visiting in August. But small zucchini, sliced and dipped in flour and then fried to a crisp, are deservedly popular in the most rarefied circles. They work as a simple first course or with cocktails or as a vegetable side dish.

> 2 small zucchini
> Flour
> Oil
> Salt

1. Peel the zucchini with a vegetable peeler. Slice off the ends and discard. Slice slantwise into thin rounds. Dump a handful of

flour into a paper bag. Drop in the zucchini and shake to coat with flour.

2. Heat oil for deep frying to about 370 degrees (see previous recipe).

3. Deep fry a teacupful of zucchini at a time until golden-brown. (Dipping the zucchini out of the bag with a teacup measures a batch and also disturbs the flour coating less than your hands would.) Drain on paper toweling.

4. Transfer finished zucchini to a serving dish, salt and serve immediately. They can be held in a low (225-degree) oven.

YIELD: 2 SERVINGS

7

FOR FOUR
OR MORE

HERE YOU WILL FIND THE CORE OF BASIC COOKING. ROAST PORK, roast chicken, ham—big pieces of meat that require relatively little attention from you but will feed a whole family or a group of friends. There are stews, pot roasts, big fish and a couple of one-pot dishes that can be expanded to sustain an army if you have a big enough pot. And there are vegetable recipes too, for vegetables that lend themselves to quantity preparation. Where possible, suggestions for using leftovers are given.

Roast Chicken

This is the easiest and best way to roast a chicken. In other books, you will find instructions about how to truss the bird and wash and season it; then how to rotate it in the oven and alter temperatures and baste it. I used to do all that, until one day I was in a great rush and I just plopped the chicken in a pan—without even inserting the canonical onion in the cavity "to remove the poisons"—and let it cook at 350 degrees for an hour. I didn't notice until I took it out to carve it that I had put it in upside down— with the breast underneath. It was fabulously juicy and tasty. The tender breast meat had been protected from the heat and hadn't dried out as it so often does when it is pointed up in the oven. And the juices from the rest of the bird had flowed downward into the breast, helping to baste it and imparting extra flavor.

1 3½-pound chicken

1. Preheat oven to 350 degrees.
2. Remove giblets and freeze for future use in **chicken stock** (see page 235). Nowadays, giblets tend to come in a little package of their own, which you'll find tucked into the cavity of the bird. Once you have it put aside, reach into the large opening of the cavity. Just at the inside edge, you will discover pouches of yellow fat. Pull them away and discard (or render for use as a cooking fat: Heat over medium heat in a saucepan until the fat melts; then strain and refrigerate).
3. Set the chicken in a roasting pan with the breast down. (The breast is the side of the chicken that both wing tips would extend toward if you pulled them; the wings grow out of the back, which is opposite the breast. The breast is fleshy—it's where the "white" meat is; the back is flattish and not fleshy.)

A rack is not necessary, although it will help prevent the skin of the bird from sticking to the pan. You could also lightly grease the pan.
4. Put the pan in the oven so that the bird is centered in the oven space. Cook for 40 minutes.

5. Loosen the breast skin of the bird from the pan with a metal spatula. With a serving fork, turn the bird over so that the breast is up. Return to the oven for 10–15 minutes. This step can be eliminated if you don't care if the breast skin is browner than it looks when you inspect it after 40 minutes of upside-down cooking. Just leave the bird in position and cook for 10–15 minutes more, as is.

6. After 50 minutes of cooking, test the chicken for doneness. The thighs are the thickest pieces and take longest to cook through. With chickens, doneness always means that juices run clear from the thickest part of the thigh when you pierce the flesh with a trussing needle or a fork. This is a convenient way of saying that the heat of cooking has transformed the blood in the flesh. The meat is cooked, i.e., not raw, when the blood isn't red anymore.

If juices don't run clear after 50 minutes of cooking, return to oven and wait another 5 or 10 minutes. That should do it.

YIELD: 4 SERVINGS

TO CARVE: Let the bird stand for a few minutes so that the flesh can firm up a bit. Then cut away the wings, drumsticks and thighs where they join the torso. The best way to do this is with poultry shears. Otherwise, secure the end of the drumstick or other piece with a fork and cut through the joint as cleanly as you can with a large knife. Once you have removed the limbs, set them aside and slice thin pieces off the breast. First, make an incision on either side of the breastbone. Then, turn the knife at an angle and slice along the contours of the rib cage, on either side of the breastbone. Carving the flesh off the rest of the carcass is a less systematic business. The back is a particularly unrewarding area, which is why backs are used for stock in restaurants. However, lurking in 2 hollow places in the bony structure of the back are 2 pouches of tender flesh called the oysters. They are often stupidly thrown away, which is why in French they are known as *sots-l'y-laissent* (fools leave them there).

LEFTOVERS: Cold roast chicken is fine eaten as is, possibly with **mayonnaise** (see page 40). Or cut up the meat and use it in a chicken salad or sandwich. Or dice it and put it in **chicken stock** (see page 235).

Poached Chicken

1 3½-pound chicken
5–6 cups chicken stock, homemade (see page 235) or canned, approximately

1. Preheat oven to 350 degrees.
2. Remove giblets and excess fat (see previous recipe).
3. Take a Dutch oven or other pot just large enough to hold the chicken and put it over a stove burner. Pour in enough chicken stock to cover the chicken (this can be done with water, but the results are inferior for obvious reasons). Test this by putting the chicken in the pot when you pour on the stock; then remove it, being careful to drain stock out of the cavity. Set the chicken aside.
4. Bring the stock to a full boil. Put the pot in the oven. Slide in the chicken, cover and poach in the oven for 45 minutes or until the juices run clear from the thigh (see previous recipe).
5. Drain the chicken. Set on a serving platter. Carve (see previous recipe). Reserve stock for future use as soup or for a repeat of this recipe.

YIELD: 4 SERVINGS

LEFTOVERS: See previous recipe.

Roast Beef

When I was a boy in the early fifties, standing rib roast was a regular event on our family's dinner table. Those were the days of cheap beef. Today's prices make this most traditional of all roasts a very special treat, but it is worth doing if you want to make an impression of opulence on guests and because of the ease and elegance of preparation and service.

>   1 6- to 8-pound standing rib roast
>   Salt
>   Pepper

1. Preheat the oven to 450 degrees.
2. Rub the meat with salt and pepper, generously. Place the roast, fat side up, on a rack in a roasting pan.
3. Set in the oven so that the thick part of the roast is in the center of the oven.
4. Cook 30 minutes. Reduce heat to 300 degrees. Continue cooking and calculate that the roast will be rare if your total cooking time is 16 to 18 minutes per pound, medium rare after 18 to 20 minutes per pound, medium after 20 to 22 minutes per pound, and well done after 26 to 30 minutes per pound. For example, a 6-pound roast, cooked rare, will take a minimum of 96 minutes, or roughly 1½ hours, a maximum of 132 minutes, or almost 2¼ hours. If you insist on well-done beef, you have a potential wait of 3 hours ahead of you (or 4 hours for an 8-pound roast).

You can finesse the arithmetic if you buy a meat thermometer. Plunge the pointed spike into the roast where it is thickest, but don't let the thermometer point hit the bone; you want the temperature of the meat, not the usually higher temperature of the bone, to read out on the dial. Beef is considered rare at 140 degrees, medium rare at 150, medium at 160 and well done at 170.

For a rolled (boneless) rib roast, the same temperature guidelines hold, but the oven temperature should be 300 degrees from the start and the cooking times are slower: 32 minutes per pound for rare, 38 minutes per pound for medium and 48 minutes per pound for well done.

YIELD: 8–12 SERVINGS

TO CARVE: Let the roast stand for 20 minutes so that it firms up. For the standing rib, start at the edge of the roast and cut long, thin slices parallel to the line of the ribs. In order to get past the ribs gracefully, use the point of the knife and free an inch or so of the meat from the bone. Then, that portion will slice easily. Continue in this manner. The rolled roast can be sliced like a salami; discard the string used for rolling before you serve the meat. Delicious juice will collect on the serving platter and should be used as a natural sauce. Spoon some on each serving as you carve.

Yorkshire pudding, a sort of savory soufflé, is a traditional accompaniment of this dish. See page 223 for a recipe.

LEFTOVERS: Roast beef sandwiches. Or serve cold slices by themselves with creamed horseradish.

Leg of Lamb

Lamb has a bad reputation in this country for two historical reasons. In the Old West, beef ranchers hated sheepmen because they put up fences and interfered with the economics and, secondarily, with the romantic ideal of open-range beef herding. The low status of sheep in our mythology spread to cities where no child ever played shepherds and Indians. Then, during World War II, GIs were force-fed nasty mutton, the overcooked meat of old ewes. This effectively turned millions of young and impressionable Americans off "lamb" (which is, properly speaking, only the meat of a sheep less than a year old). The lamb industry has been in decline in the United States for decades, but American lamb is greatly superior in quality to cheaper frozen lamb from New Zealand. To avoid a muttony taste, it is essential not to overcook lamb. The flesh should be served pink.

> 1 6-pound leg of lamb
> 6 potatoes, peeled (see page 159) and cut into 1-inch cubes

1. Preheat oven to 450 degrees.

2. Set the lamb in a rack in a roasting pan. Push a meat thermometer, if you have one, into the thickest part of the lamb, but not far enough to hit the bone. Cook 15 minutes.

3. Reduce heat to 350 degrees. Scatter the potato cubes on the bottom of the pan. Cook another 45 minutes, turning the potatoes once or twice along the way. The lamb is done if the thermometer reads 150 degrees and/or the juices run pink, not red. If you aren't sure, cook another 15 minutes. Little will be lost by this and, although pink lamb is the only way to go—160-degree, well-done lamb tastes rank and is the reason why most Americans who have only tasted it that way hate lamb—raw lamb is no picnic.

4. Remove the lamb to a serving platter and let it rest, to firm up, for 20 minutes. Check the potatoes. If they aren't done, spoon pan juices over them and return to the oven until 5 minutes before you are ready to carve the lamb.

5. Remove the potatoes to a serving bowl with a slotted spoon. Cover to keep warm.

6. Pour excess fat out of the pan. Strain remaining juices, reserve and pour over potatoes just before you serve them, or pass separately.

YIELD: 6 SERVINGS

TO CARVE: Cut a flat place on the bottom of the leg (the side that has the least meat and is closest to the bone). Use this as a steadying point. Stick a carving fork into the fleshy part of the leg. Use the fork to hold the leg steady while you slice. Now make one slice along the bone, to release the main section of meat from the bone. Next, cut a series of thin slices perpendicular to the first cut. In effect, you are carving the choicest part of the leg as if it were a loaf of bread. After you have finished with this section, you will have to improvise the rest, cutting slices where you find them.

LEFTOVERS: If you like cold lamb, you can make sandwiches. Otherwise, chop fine or grind to make patties seasoned with salt, pepper and ground cumin; then sauté in oil until browned and heated through.

Pork Roast

This is the best value, in terms of both cost and convenience, of all the major meat dishes. The insertion of garlic cloves into the meat enhances the flavor of the whole roast. Rosemary is the spice of preference; it marries with pork to perfection.

> 1 4- to 5-pound pork roast (with bone)
> 6 garlic cloves, peeled (see page 43)
>   Dried rosemary
>   Salt
>   Pepper
> ¼ cup heavy cream

1. Preheat oven to 325 degrees.
2. Cut the garlic cloves lengthwise into slivers that are thin but not so thin that they won't hold their shape.
3. Take a small work knife and jab its point into the flesh of the roast in several places, cutting in 1 or 2 inches. Into each of these pockets, insert a sliver of garlic; they will slide in and disappear. Rub salt and pepper into the meat, generously. Place on a rack in a roasting pan (the rack is not essential). Sprinkle all over

with rosemary. Place the pan in the oven and go about your business, returning every ½ hour to baste the roast.

4. After 2 hours (2½ if the roast is a boneless, rolled roast), check for doneness by cutting into the thickest part of the roast. The meat should be moist and white, not pink.

5. Place the roast on a serving platter. Pour off most of the fat in the roasting pan. Pour in the heavy cream and bring to a boil with the pan juices. Scrape the pan bottom with a metal spatula to deglaze the meat juices that have adhered to it. Pour through a strainer into a sauce boat.

YIELD: 6–8 SERVINGS

TO CARVE: Proceed immediately, slicing between the ribs. The butcher will most likely have broken the main bone at appropriate points to make it easier for you to cut completely through and create a set of neat pork chops. Rolled roasts can be carved like salamis; remember to set aside the string used for rolling.

LEFTOVERS: Serve as cold chops with mustard. Or cut away all bones and fat and slice for sandwiches.

Ham Braised in Madeira

Sugar-glazed ham is an anachronism and a waste of time. You can serve ham as a hot main course for a large crowd in a much more elegant way and with less trouble if you follow this classic method of southwest France.

All hams are already cooked in one way or another—smoked, cured in salt—unless they are sold as fresh ham. This is a recipe for normal American smoked, cured ham. It is not appropriate for a salty—and delicious—country ham. Don't try it on Italian prosciutto or other unsmoked "raw" hams meant to be sliced and eaten as cold cuts. It is also not something worth trying with a canned ham, because canned hams, which look like the can they came in, shouldn't be served whole on a table. Buy a whole ham, cured and smoked, with the bone in. You will also have to have a Dutch oven or turkey roaster big enough to hold the entire ham, covered.

This is a quite economical way to feed a lot of people at once, economical in money and in time. It turns an ordinary supermarket ham into a very special piece of meat.

1 8- to 10-pound smoked and cured ham
2 cups Madeira wine

1. Preheat oven to 275 degrees.
2. Trim the ham of almost all its fat. Leave a ½-inch layer.
3. Set the ham in a roaster or other pot that will just hold it, covered.
4. Add the Madeira and bring to a boil on top of the stove.
5. Cover and cook in oven for 2 hours. The ham is done when it slices easily.
6. Using a large carving fork, preferably 2, lift the ham out of its pot. Let it drain and set on a carving board or a serving platter. Let it rest for ½ hour. Then slice it and serve with a **rice pilaf** (see page 195). (The cooking liquid is too salty to use in a sauce, but the Madeira left in the bottle will keep indefinitely, unrefrigerated.)

YIELD: 10 SERVINGS

TO CARVE: Make a long slice along the bone, steadying the ham with a fork if necessary. Then make a series of slices perpendicular to the first cut, as if you were slicing a loaf of bread. The ham gives you many opportunities to do this along its bounteous bone.

LEFTOVERS: Eternity, the saying goes, is two people and a ham; but it is an eternity of tasty ham sandwiches (also, salads with ham strips in them and scrambled eggs with diced ham mixed in).

Pot Roast

Like all pot roasts, this recipe, based on an Italian dish called *stra-còtto*, makes big chunks of meat tender through gradual cooking immersed in a flavored liquid in a pot. You do not have to use an unglazed terra-cotta pot, but it dramatically improves the flavor of the result. Pot roast tastes better the second day, after the flavors of the cooking liquid have time to permeate the meat. Reheating does no damage at all to the dish. Obviously, this means that you can prepare pot roast well in advance of serving.

> 3 pounds beef round or chuck all in one piece
> Salt
> Pepper
> 2 cloves garlic, minced (see page 43)
> 1 small onion, finely chopped (see page 39)
> 1 tablespoon oil
> 1 tablespoon butter
> 2 bay leaves
> 2 cups dry red wine
> 1 large can Italian tomatoes
> 1 8-ounce can tomato sauce

1. Season meat with salt and pepper.

2. Sauté onion and garlic in a large heavy skillet in oil and butter until onion is translucent. Push to the side of the skillet. Add meat and cook over high heat until well browned on all sides. Browning occurs when the hot pan seizes the meat. In other words, the meat is supposed to stick to the pan. High heat is essential. So is holding the meat on its side to sear it there too. Remove from heat as soon as browning is complete.

3. Transfer meat to a large pot. (It will taste better if you use an unglazed terra-cotta pot. The one most commonly available is sold as Romertopf. Soak it in cold water before using.) Add bay leaves and wine, bring to a boil, then reduce heat so that the liquid simmers. Cook this way for 20 minutes, uncovered. (If you

are using terra-cotta, you must protect it from the direct flame with an asbestos pad.)

4. Add tomatoes and their liquid along with tomato sauce. Cover and continue simmering for 3 hours. Uncover during the last ½ hour to allow the sauce to evaporate and thicken. You should end up with about 5 cups of sauce.

YIELD: 6 SERVINGS

LEFTOVERS: Pot roast is better the second day, after gentle reheating.

Beef Stew

You could say that a stew is really a pot roast for which the meat has been cut into small cubes. This vastly multiplies the surface area available for browning. Browning improves the flavor and color of the cooking liquid, which ultimately becomes the sauce for the meat. Ergo, careful browning is the name of the game. Stew meat tends to be cheap and is a route to the convenient feeding of crowds.

3 large onions, finely chopped (see page 39)
3 tablespoons oil
2 pounds round of beef, cut into 2-inch cubes
   Salt
   Pepper
2 sprigs parsley
1 bay leaf
½ teaspoon dried thyme
3 large potatoes, peeled and quartered
4 medium carrots, peeled and quartered

1. Sauté onions in oil until translucent.
2. Remove onions to a plate. Brown the beef cubes, a handful

at a time, over high heat (see previous recipe). Turn the cubes so that each face of each cube is well browned. If you put in too many cubes at once, the heat will be reduced and this task will take forever. As each cube is finished, remove it to a bowl and add another until all the cubes are browned.

3. Put onions and beef in a large pot. Cover with water. Add salt, pepper, parsley, bay leaf and thyme. Bring to a boil, reduce heat and simmer, covered, for 2 hours or until meat is tender but not stringy.

4. Add potatoes and carrots and simmer for another 30 minutes, uncovered.

YIELD: 6 SERVINGS

LEFTOVERS: Like most stews, this one improves the second day, when slowly reheated.

Picadillo

Picadillo is the most interesting thing I know to do with ground beef. It is spicy; it is quick. You can double or triple this recipe, reheat it, freeze it, alter the spices. It always works.

    2 pounds ground beef chuck
    3 large onions, chopped (see page 39)
    1 green bell pepper, chopped (see page 44)
    2 tablespoons cumin
      Salt
      Pepper
    1 teaspoon Cayenne pepper

1. Put the ground beef in a large skillet and cook over medium heat, turning the meat so that all the little pieces are exposed to the heat.

2. After a bit, the meat will release its fat. Then add the on-

ion and green pepper. Mix into the meat and continue cooking until the onion and green pepper have softened.

3. Stir in remaining ingredients and raise the heat to high. Try to brown all the beef granules, stirring regularly.

YIELD: 4–6 SERVINGS

LEFTOVERS: This improves with age and reheating: the spices permeate the meat more thoroughly after a night spent together.

New Mexico Chili

No beans, no tomatoes—that's the trademark of real southwestern chili. You could use a prepared chili powder, but almost any ethnic-food store sells some kind of fresh chili peppers these days, so why not do it right?

> 4 **pounds lean beef, cut into 2-inch cubes**
> 2 **tablespoons lard (for New Mexican authenticity) or oil**
> 2 **large onions, chopped (see page 39)**
> 2 **garlic cloves, finely chopped (see page 43)**
> ½ **teaspoon dried oregano**
> 2 **cups fresh green chilies, chopped (or less if you don't think you're up to the heat),** *or* 1 **tablespoon Cayenne pepper, approximately**
> ½ **teaspoon cumin**
> **Salt**

1. Brown the beef cubes in the lard or oil (see previous recipe) in a large pot. Remove the cubes as they brown and reserve. After the last batch is done, let the heat of the lard reduce. Then add the onions and garlic and sauté until the onions are translucent.

Return the beef to the pot. Add water to cover. Bring to a boil and add all remaining ingredients except salt. Reduce heat and simmer uncovered for 2 hours or until beef is tender but not stringy. Salt to taste and serve.

YIELD: 8 SERVINGS

LEFTOVERS: This dish is infinitely reheatable.

Big Fish

Different kinds of fish taste different from each other, but there are very few methods of fish cookery that work for only one variety. What matters is the size of the fish and whether it is going to be cooked whole, filleted or in steaks. Here are two basic methods for dealing with whole fish of substantial size.

Baked Fish

1 4- to 5-pound whole, fleshy fish (such as sea bass, red snapper or weakfish), scaled and gutted, but with head and tail left on
Salt
6 tablespoons butter, melted

1. Preheat oven to 400 degrees.
2. Spread a double layer of aluminum foil over an oven-proof pan large enough to hold the fish. The aluminum foil should extend out beyond the pan at both ends. Grease the part of the top of the foil that lies over the pan.
3. Set the fish on the greased foil. Sprinkle with salt. Brush the top of the fish with 4 tablespoons of the butter.

4. Bake the fish in the oven for 30 to 40 minutes, until the flesh flakes easily with a fork. Brush on more butter every 10 minutes.

5. Remove pan from oven. Drain butter out of foil with baster or spoon. Grasp ends of foil and raise fish from pan. Slide it off the foil onto a serving dish, taking care not to damage the fish, which is quite breakable at this point.

YIELD: 8 SERVINGS

TO CARVE: Cut off head and tail. Make an incision through the skin along the crest of the back; this is merely to separate the top and bottom halves of the skin. Now run the flat of the knife through your first cut and between the top flesh and the backbone. Working gently, separate the entire top half of the fish from the skeleton. Next, you can cut straight down into the top flesh, to create serving pieces, which you lift out with the flat of the knife. When you've served all the flesh on the top side of the fish, pull away the skeleton, working the flat of the knife between the bones and the bottom flesh, if necessary. Discard the bones and continue dividing the bottom flesh.

LEFTOVERS: Serve cold in a salad, with **vinaigrette dressing** (see page 53), **mayonnaise** (see page 40) or just lemon juice.

Poached Fish

You could, of course, poach a fish in plain water and in any kind of pot that would hold it. But the fish will taste better if it is poached in a flavored liquid, known officially as a court bouillon (freezable and reusable). And the convenience of a true fish poacher is great. It is long and narrow, just the right shape to hold a fish plus the bare minimum of liquid necessary to cook it. And it has a perforated rack with handles, so that you can remove the fish from the poacher without violence while the liquid drains back into the poacher through the holes in the rack. If you aren't sure how long to poach a fish, measure its breadth at its thickest point. Figure 10 minutes per inch.

1¼ cups vinegar
1 carrot, peeled and diced
½ teaspoon dried thyme
1 tablespoon salt
1 bay leaf
2 onions, chopped (see page 39)
1 3-pound fleshy fish, such as salmon or mackerel, scaled and gutted, but with head and tail left on

1. Add vinegar, carrot, thyme, salt, bay leaf and onion to 4 quarts water in a large saucepan. Boil, reduce heat and simmer for 1 hour, uncovered. Let cool. Strain.

2. Pour the strained liquid (court bouillon) into the fish poacher. Arrange the fish on the rack of the poacher and lower into cold court bouillon.

3. Set the poacher over medium heat and let liquid come to a boil. Immediately reduce heat and simmer slowly for about 25 minutes or until the flesh flakes easily.

4. Raise the rack, let the fish drain and then transfer it to a serving platter.

YIELD: 6 SERVINGS

TO CARVE: See previous recipe.

LEFTOVERS: See previous recipe.

Vegetables

Cauliflower

Mark Twain said that cauliflower is a cabbage with a college education. This is amusing but false. Cauliflower is genetically the same plant as broccoli and kale, but it is cultivated to produce an immense white sphere of flowerets. This is the classic preparation. Cook it in winter, when more obviously glamorous vegetables are out of season, expensive and poor in quality. Your cauliflower will not have the mildewed taste you remember from oversteamed institutional cauliflower.

1 medium cauliflower
4 tablespoons butter
2 tablespoons bread crumbs

1. Trim off the green leaves. Then put the cauliflower in a pot large enough to hold it. Add water to a depth of 2 inches.
2. Bring to a boil, reduce heat, cover and simmer until the thick base of the cauliflower is tender, about 10 minutes.
3. Meanwhile, melt the butter in a skillet and sauté the bread crumbs until they are toasted, stirring.
4. Remove the cauliflower to a serving bowl. Pour butter and bread crumbs over the top.

YIELD: 4–6 SERVINGS

LEFTOVERS: Puree in a processor or blender. Reheat with a small amount of butter.

Squash

It is patriotic to eat squash, which is a New World vegetable. Squash is also a sensible vegetable for the working person, because it keeps well at room temperature, for a week at least, and it requires almost no handwork.

> 1 large Hubbard or butternut or 3 medium acorn squash
> 8 tablespoons (4 ounces) butter
> 3 tablespoons brown sugar
> ½ teaspoon salt

1. Preheat oven to 375 degrees.

2. Cut the squash in half. Scrape out the seeds and discard them. Place squash, cut sides up, in a roasting pan.

3. Melt 3 tablespoons butter and brush over tops of squash. If using acorn squash, sprinkle with brown sugar.

4. Bake 40 minutes or until tender.

5. Serve acorn squash immediately, one half-squash per person. With other varieties, spoon the flesh out of the shells and puree in a processor, food mill or blender, combining with remaining butter, brown sugar and salt.

YIELD: 6 SERVINGS

LEFTOVERS: Transfer pureed squash to a greased baking dish and reheat in 375-degree oven for 20 minutes.

Rice

Some varieties of rice need to be washed before cooking; others do not. Always read the package. This is an all-purpose recipe for plain steamed white rice.

>   1 cup raw rice
>   1 tablespoon butter
>   1 teaspoon salt

1. Combine all ingredients with 2 cups water in a medium saucepan.

2. Bring water to a boil over high heat. Reduce heat as low as it will go, stir the rice once, cover pan and simmer for 12 minutes or until all liquid is absorbed by the rice and the rice is tender but not mushy.

YIELD: 4 SERVINGS

LEFTOVERS: Combine with olive oil, vinegar, ¼ cup chopped onion and 1 tablespoon fresh, or 1 teaspoon dried, tarragon (add 1 tablespoon chopped parsley if using dried tarragon) to make a cold rice salad.

8

VEGETABLE
LOVE

*"My vegetable love should grow
Vaster than empires . . ."*
—ANDREW MARVELL, "To His Coy Mistress"

CONSIDER, FOR A MOMENT, THE IDEAL TOMATO. IT IS BOLD RED, so ripe it tests the sharpest knife, so nicely balanced in taste between natural sugar and natural acid that it tests your palate—and excites it—like a complex wine.

Fresh, seasonal vegetables of all kinds are just as splendid and extraordinary as the tomato. And it is one of the noteworthy developments of the past twenty years that large numbers of people have come to value vegetables at their true worth. We are no longer a country that laughs at spinach or spurns lettuce as decoration for solid "real" food. Behind the risen status of all vegetables in our time are many causes ranging from the natural-foods movement to straightforward vegetarianism prompted by ecological, sentimental and religious concerns. While most people have still not turned vegetarian, millions have edged in that direction and learned to love vegetables with the passion of new converts. For whatever initial reason, they—we—have begun to put vegetables at the center of our food thinking.

For the cook, this new openness to vegetables offers almost unlimited opportunities for variety. In an atmosphere where asparagus has become a glamour food, even the turnip and the kohlrabi may soon get the respect they deserve.

In this chapter you will find a selection of dishes that can be combined to make all-vegetable meals or prepared separately as appetizers, main dishes and side dishes. There are, of course, many other vegetable dishes in this book. Those below both round out the list and also give you a convenient place to look when you want to prepare a nonmeat meal for vegetarian guests or for yourself, when you are smitten with vegetable love.

First Courses

Corn on the Cob

Supermarkets these days seem to begin selling corn on the cob in late February. No serious person buys corn except when it is in season locally. This usually means the high summer, July 4 at the earliest. Purists will only eat corn picked the day they eat it. They know that the sweetness of sweet corn declines abruptly from the moment it is separated from the stalk. Corn fanatics start water boiling, then go out into the cornfield, pick their ears and race home to boil them as quickly as humanly possible. This is excessive, but you get the point. With corn on the cob, freshness is all.

> 12 **ears corn on the cob, unshucked**
>   **Salt**
> 1 **stick butter at room temperature**

1. Bring 6 quarts water to a full, rolling boil in a pot large enough to hold the water and the corn.

2. While the water comes to the boil, shuck the corn. Pull the husks off, rub away any residual strands of cornsilk and snap off any pieces of stalk. It is best to do this job outdoors, if you can, since it creates a pile of debris. Be prepared with a bag for collecting it all.

3. When the water boils, add ⅓ cup salt and then put in the corn. Very fresh, very sweet corn should be done almost as soon as the water returns to the boil. It will not, in any case, take very much time to turn ideally tender. After all, you could eat it raw in a pinch. To test, remove an ear with tongs and take a bite. Save that ear for yourself.

4. To serve, pile all the ears on a large platter and bring to the table with salt and butter. Everyone has his own way of but-

tering corn. I prefer rolling the ear against a stick of butter. However you do it, put the butter on first, then sprinkle the salt. The butter makes the salt stick to the corn.

YIELD: 4–5 SERVINGS

Ratatouille

In Nice, other parts of the south of France, and more recently all over the world where people have come to know this stew of eggplant, onion and tomatoes, ratatouille (ra-ta-too-ee) is a favorite cold appetizer or side dish. It can be served hot too, or reheated. Once you get the basic idea, you can alter the proportions to suit the availability of ingredients or your taste. Some people add sliced zucchini; I think that adds nothing but bulk. Everyone uses olive oil, the tonic note of this vegetable scale. Do not overcook. The eggplant and pepper slices should hold their shape, tender but not mushy.

> 2 large eggplants, unpeeled, cut into ¼-inch cubes
> Salt
> 2 large tomatoes, if fresh, or 4 canned whole Italian plum tomatoes
> 2 red (or green) bell peppers
> ⅓ cup olive oil
> 2 large onions, peeled and sliced thin
> 2 cloves garlic, finely chopped (see page 43)
> 1 teaspoon coriander seeds

1. Sprinkle eggplant cubes lightly with salt and put in a colander. Place the colander in the sink. Set a plate over the eggplant and weight it so as to press excess liquid out of it. Leave for an hour or so and prepare the other vegetables.

2. If you are using fresh tomatoes, plunge them, one at a time, in boiling water for 10 seconds. Remove with a slotted spoon. Cut out the stem and then pull away the peel. This will be simple now that they have been blanched in boiling water. Then cut them in half at the equator (consider the stem as the north pole). Squeeze gently to extract seeds and excess juice. Chop roughly and reserve in a bowl.

If you use canned tomatoes, both blanching and skinning have been done for you by the canner.

3. Cut out the stems of the peppers. Red peppers are sweeter and work better in this recipe. Either red or green peppers should be cut in half. Then discard seeds, cut away interior white flesh, discard, and slice peppers into thin strips.

4. In a large skillet, heat the olive oil until an onion ring tossed into it sizzles immediately. Add the remaining onion. The slices will separate into rings as you stir them with a wooden spoon. Cook until translucent (do not brown). Straightaway, add eggplant, pepper and garlic. Cover, lower heat and cook slowly for 40 minutes. The oil should barely bubble.

5. Meanwhile, grind the coriander seeds to the consistency you get with peppercorns from a pepper mill. This can be done easily with a mortar and pestle if you have one. Or simply put the seeds on a cutting board and use the bottom of a bottle, pressing and rotating. This job can be done in a blender, but it doesn't seem worth it to me to haul out the machine and then clean it.

6. After 40 minutes of cooking the eggplant mixture, add the tomato and the coriander. Cover again and cook slowly another 20 minutes or until all the vegetables are soft but not mushy. Taste. Add salt and pepper to taste. Serve hot or cold. In a nonvegetarian context, ratatouille goes very nicely as a side dish with meat.

YIELD: 6 SERVINGS

Corn Chowder

You have to make this soup in the summer, when you can buy fresh corn on the cob. But you can freeze it for cooler weather. This makes real sense if you prepare a significant quantity of the soup at one time, say triple the recipe below. You'll want to eat some immediately, of course.

  4 cups milk, approximately
  2 onion slices
  4 ears corn, shucked (see page 187)
  4 tablespoons all-purpose flour
    Salt
    Pepper

1. Heat three cups milk and the onion slices over medium-low heat in a 4-quart saucepan. Keep an eye on this. When milk boils, it foams up dramatically and can overflow the pot. So lower heat or remove the pot from the burner if the milk begins to boil. It should not get that far if you move on directly to the next step.

2. With the point of a sharp knife, slit all the corn kernels down the middle. Run the knife lengthwise along the rows of kernels. Then, press the kernels with the back of the knife to force out the contents of the kernels into a bowl. Leave the skins of the kernels attached to the cobs. Discard the cobs.

3. When the milk starts to steam, fish out the onion slices with tongs or a slotted spoon and discard. Then stir the corn mush from the bowl into the milk. Cook over moderate heat for 10 minutes. Do not boil.

4. At this point, you have three choices. You can serve the soup as is. You can thin it out with some or all of the remaining milk. Or you can thicken it with a slurry (a mixture of a flour or other pulverized substance dissolved in a liquid) of the 4 tablespoons of flour blended with the remaining milk. The way I learned to make this, one did add the flour-milk slurry, and I think most people will prefer the thicker soup. But you should at least con-

sider not doing this before you mix up the slurry in a bowl and pour a cup of the hot soup into it and then return the mixture to the soup pot. Stir as mixture thickens. Cook 5 or 6 minutes longer, without boiling, until the flour loses any raw taste. Season with salt and pepper to taste.

YIELD: 4–6 SERVINGS

Artichoke Soup

This is not an everyday soup. Scraping the leaves of 4 artichokes is toilsome. But for people you like, the taste is so extraordinary you will want to go to the trouble now and then. It is essential to go through the fine-straining stage in order to eliminate the artichoke flesh's fibers and produce a silken texture. The conical chinois strainer is ideal for this job. Stores that sell them will also sell a wooden tool, called a champignon because of its fluted, spherical knob, that helps force the liquid through the chinois. You work it up and down in the soup, agitating the soup and accelerating its slow passage through the fine metal mesh of the chinois.

4 medium artichokes
1 lemon
6 tablespoons butter
6 cups chicken stock, approximately (see page 235)
2 cups potatoes, sliced thickly
  Salt
  Pepper

1. Cut artichokes in half vertically. Cut lemon in half. Rub all cut surfaces of artichokes with the cut surface of the lemon. (The acid in the lemon counteracts the blackening effect that content with air has on cut artichokes.) With a small knife, cut out

the hairy chokes located in a pouch just above the fleshy artichoke bottoms. Discard the choke fibers and rub the cut surfaces of the artichokes with the lemon.

2. Melt the butter in a 6-quart saucepan over medium-high heat. Add the artichoke halves and toss to coat with butter. Add 3 cups of the stock and 3 cups water and bring to a boil. Reduce heat, cover and simmer for 30 minutes.

3. Add potato slices and cook about 20 more minutes, or until potatoes are tender. Then, using a slotted spoon, remove artichokes to a bowl. Remove potato slices to another bowl. Strain and reserve the cooking liquid.

4. Scrape all edible material from each artichoke leaf with a silver or stainless steel spoon and add to potatoes.

5. Trim the artichoke bottoms and add to the potatoes and leaf scrapings. Then add the reserved cooking liquid.

6. Puree the mixture in batches in a blender or processor. Then push through a chinois or other fine-mesh strainer.

7. Stir in as much of the remaining stock as you think is necessary to create a desirable consistency. I prefer this soup on the light side and would normally use all the stock. The taste is strong enough to survive dilution handily and the thinner texture is a bit more elegant. Season with salt and pepper. Serve hot or cold.

YIELD: 4 SERVINGS

Main Dishes

Grape Leaves Stuffed with Tabbouleh

Every Middle Eastern cuisine has at least one recipe for grape leaves. If you have ever lived near a grapevine, you will understand why people want to use the multitude of leaves that are left after the grapes have been picked. It is very easy to prepare fresh leaves (boil in lightly salted water for a minute or two), but I have done this and see no particular advantage over preserved leaves, unless you have a vine in the vicinity. This quite delicious recipe is inspired by a specialty of Armenia, to my mind the place where the standard ideas of Middle Eastern cooking reach their height. Tabbouleh is a prepared form of wheat also known as bulgur and is sold almost everywhere. After steeping in hot water, it emerges slightly crunchy, slightly chewy and has a strong personality. It can be served cold, mixed with plenty of chopped mint. This more elaborate dish adds various dried fruits as well as chopped herbs and, of course, the mildly sour envelope of grape leaves. Perfection on a summer night. No forks necessary.

> 1¼ cups coarse tabbouleh (bulgur wheat)
> ¾ cup oil
> 1 large onion, finely chopped (see page 39)
> 6 prunes, pitted and finely chopped
> ½ cup raisins
> ½ cup chopped mint leaves
> Salt
> Pepper
> 1 1-pound jar preserved grape leaves

1. Soak the tabbouleh in hot water to cover for ½ hour. Then drain in a large strainer and reserve in a mixing bowl.

2. Meanwhile, heat ¼ cup oil in a large skillet. Sauté onion until lightly browned. To avoid burning, stir frequently and remove from heat as soon as browning begins. Cooking will continue in the pan, so quickly pour the onion and oil into the mixing bowl and stir together with tabbouleh.

3. Now stir in the chopped prunes, raisins, mint leaves, salt and pepper.

4. Rinse grape leaves. Dry on paper toweling.

5. Now begin stuffing the leaves. Take a leaf, cut off any protruding remnant of stem and lay it down with the dull side up. Put a tablespoon or so of stuffing on the leaf near the stem end. Roll the stem end over the stuffing. Now fold the sides of the leaf over the stuffing and roll up the leaf, starting from the stem end. Continue in this manner until you have used up all the stuffing. You should produce about 50 little cylindrical packages. Stack them in layers in a casserole or Dutch oven, leaving the seams facing down to prevent unrolling as you put them in and during cooking.

6. Mix the remaining ½ cup oil with a cup of water and pour over the stuffed leaves.

7. Bring to a boil, reduce heat and cover. After a minute or so, check to see that the liquid is bubbling gently. Re-cover and simmer for 50 minutes. The stuffing should be rather soft, but if you crave a chewier texture, begin testing after 40 minutes. It is also a good idea to inspect the casserole after ½ hour just to make sure that the liquid has not been absorbed. Add more water if necessary.

8. Remove the stuffed leaves and set them in a single layer on a large platter so that they will cool quickly and uniformly. Serve at room temperature.

YIELD: 5 SERVINGS AS A MAIN COURSE,
10 AS AN APPETIZER OR IN COMBINATION WITH OTHER DISHES

Rice Pilaf

Italians might call this a risotto. But the fundamental method of cooking rice suggested here seems to have come from the Orient at some point and spread to several cuisines, even to the regional cooking of the American Southeast, under various forms of the word *pilaf* (*pilau, perloo*). Escoffier, the greatest of the old *haute cuisine* chefs, had his version. The world is full of them.

Fundamentally, we are all talking about rice quickly sautéed and then cooked in chicken stock instead of water (strict vegetarians can get quite reasonable results substituting water for chicken stock, but the rich taste will be missing). The grains swell by imbibing the stock. Then other solid ingredients are added to make a substantial dish. You will get the best results with a short-grain rice from Italy's Po Valley, sold as Arborio rice in specialty shops. It does not turn so easily to mush. But I have had quite reasonable results with American long-grain rice and with fragrant basmati rice from India.

½ **pound (2 sticks) butter**
1 **large onion, chopped (see page 39)**
5 **cups chicken stock (see page 235)**
2 **cups raw rice, preferably Arborio**
3 **canned Italian tomatoes, drained, seeded and chopped**
20 **mushroom caps, sautéed in 2 tablespoons butter until tender**
Flowerets from 1 broccoli
Salt
Pepper

1. Melt the butter in a heavy 6-quart saucepan.

2. Heat over medium heat until foam subsides and then add onion. Sauté until onion is transparent. Meanwhile, bring stock to a boil in another saucepan.

3. Pour the rice in a steady stream into the big saucepan with

the butter and onion. Stir constantly until the rice turns milky. This happens almost right away. Then pour in the boiling stock. Cover and cook over low heat for 10 minutes.

4. Stir tomatoes, mushroom caps and broccoli flowerets into rice. Cover and continue cooking over low heat another 10 minutes or until rice is *al dente* (see page 143). Remove from heat and let stand, covered, until any remaining liquid has been absorbed.

YIELD: 8 SERVINGS

Lasagne with Mushrooms

This is a very pure, tomatoless northern Italian form of lasagne, the baked classic dish formed from alternating layers of long, wide pasta strips, ricotta and mozzarella cheese, sauce and, usually, ground meat and tomato sauce. Here mushrooms substitute for the meat, making for a subtler, more focused taste.

Salt
Oil
1 pound lasagne
¼ cup olive oil
1 clove garlic, finely chopped (see page 43)
2 pounds fresh mushrooms, wiped clean and sliced
¼ teaspoon dried oregano
½ cup dry white wine
2 cups milk
4 tablespoons (½ stick) butter
5 tablespoons flour
1 cup grated Parmesan or Romano cheese

1. Bring 6 quarts of water to a boil in a large pot. When the water boils, add 1 tablespoon salt, 1 tablespoon of any cooking oil

and the lasagne. Cook for about 10 minutes or until *al dente* (see page 143). Drain in a colander and reserve.

2. While the lasagne is boiling, heat the olive oil over moderate heat in a large skillet. After a couple minutes, drop a speck of garlic into the oil. The oil is ready when the garlic sizzles. Add the rest of the garlic and the mushroom slices. Toss them in the oil for a minute or two. Then add oregano and wine. Bring to a boil, then lower heat until the liquid barely bubbles. Cook until almost all the liquid has evaporated, about 15 minutes. Stir from time to time.

3. If you work efficiently, you can prepare a béchamel sauce while the mushrooms are cooking. First bring the milk to the boiling point in a medium saucepan. Don't let it fully boil as it will erupt in a vaporous wave and overflow. Remove from heat and set aside. Then melt the butter over medium-low heat in a small skillet. After the foam subsides, stir in the flour very thoroughly. You will get a smooth paste that is called a roux. For béchamel, the quintessential white sauce, you cook the roux for only 2 or 3 minutes. Do not brown. Then whisk the roux into the milk vigorously, eliminating all lumps. Put the sauce over medium heat and cook, whisking regularly for 5 minutes. Set aside.

4. Preheat oven to 375 degrees.

5. Assemble the lasagne in a baking pan of 8-cup capacity. The classic lasagne-pan dimensions are approximately 14 by 8 inches with straight sides rising 2 to 3 inches high. Grease the bottom and sides with oil. Then spread a layer of lasagne strips over the bottom. Spread about ¼ of the béchamel over the lasagne. Then sprinkle with ¼ cup grated cheese. Then spread about ⅓ of the mushrooms. Repeat this process twice more. Then cover with a fourth layer of lasagne strips and top with the remaining béchamel and grated cheese.

6. Bake for 20 minutes or until the top of the lasagne has browned lightly. To serve, cut in rectangles.

YIELD: 6 SERVINGS

Rigatoni Primavera

Primavera is Italian for spring. Pasta primavera is garnished with several spring vegetables. In the myriad restaurants where you will find this dish, they too often choose an extremely delicate type of noodle, such as the aptly named *capelli d'angelo* (angel's hair). In fact, what is required is a noodle that will not be overpowered by its sturdier vegetable companions. If you can't find the corrugated tubes called rigatoni, at least buy a pasta of substantial size.

> Salt
> Oil
> 1 pound rigatoni
> 1 clove garlic, finely chopped (see page 43)
> 1 scallion, trimmed and chopped (both white and green parts)
> ½ cup carrot, peeled and chopped
> 1 medium zucchini, washed, seeded and diced
> 2 large fresh tomatoes, blanched, skinned, seeded and chopped (see page 189)
> ½ cup shelled fresh peas, simmered for 3 minutes in boiling lightly salted water and drained
> Grated Parmesan cheese

1. Bring 6 quarts of water to a boil in a large pot. When the water boils, add a tablespoon of salt and a tablespoon of oil. Then add rigatoni. Boil uncovered for 10 minutes or until the rigatoni are *al dente* (see page 143).

2. Meanwhile, heat 3 tablespoons of oil in a large skillet over medium-high heat. When a piece of garlic dropped into the oil sizzles, add the scallion, carrot and zucchini. Sauté for 5 minutes or until softened but not mushy. Add tomato and cook another 2 minutes.

3. Toss rigatoni with mixture from step 2 and the reserved peas. If all the cooking is done at approximately the same time,

all ingredients should be hot. Serve immediately, passing grated Parmesan.

YIELD: 4 SERVINGS

Ragout of Barley

Barley is an unfairly neglected grain. It used to be the staple for northern cultures that couldn't raise wheat. Barley meal makes a very sustaining flat bread. You can even make a kind of "rice pudding" with barley. This vegetable stew acquires its personality from barley's special taste and chewy texture.

>Salt
1½ cups pearled barley
¼ cup any cooking oil except olive oil
2 medium carrots, peeled and sliced into thin rounds
2 ribs celery, trimmed and chopped
1 green bell pepper, stemmed, seeded and chopped (see page 44)
1 large onion, chopped (see page 39)
½ pound mushrooms, wiped clean and sliced
>Pepper

1. Bring 3 cups water to a boil in a 4-quart saucepan.
2. Add salt and barley. When water boils again, reduce heat to low, cover and simmer for 40 minutes or until the barley is *al dente* (see page 143).
3. Meanwhile, heat oil in a large skillet over medium heat. Test after a couple minutes by dropping in a carrot round. When the oil sizzles on contact with the carrot, add the rest of the rounds and sauté for 5 minutes, stirring so as to coat all the rounds with oil and produce even cooking.
4. Add celery, pepper and onion. Sauté as above until the onion is translucent. Then add mushrooms. Sauté until all vegetables

have softened to the point you like, but don't overdo it and let them get mushy. If the mushrooms release water (you'll know because the cooking liquid will boil and let off steam), continue cooking until it evaporates.

5. Drain barley in a colander and transfer to a serving dish. Stir in the vegetables from the skillet. Season with salt and pepper to taste.

YIELD: 6 SERVINGS

Lo Han Chai

This is a well-known Chinese mixed-vegetable dish. Since some of the ingredients have to be bought in your local Chinatown or at a specialty market, you might as well do all the shopping there. (If you have a wok, use it instead of the skillet specified below. But frankly I can see no reason for buying a wok for home cooking. Stir-frying of modest quantities can be done just as well in a skillet.) The mixture of ingredients in lo han chai shows genius. This is easier to do than it may look, especially if you arrange all the ingredients within easy reach of the stove before the final cooking stage.

> 6 Chinese black mushrooms
> 1 canned bamboo shoot, diced
> 1 potato, peeled and diced
> ½ carrot, scraped and diced
> ½ cup cauliflower flowerets
> 1 cucumber, peeled, seeded and diced
> ½ cup rice noodles
> 5 tablespoons peanut oil
> 10 mushrooms
> 12 quail eggs, boiled for 5 minutes and shelled
> 10 pieces canned baby corn

1 cup chicken stock (see page 235)
3 tablespoons soy sauce
1 teaspoon salt
1 teaspoon sugar
2 teaspoons sesame oil

1. Soak black mushrooms in warm water for 15 minutes. Then cut away stems and discard. Set trimmed black mushrooms aside.

2. Meanwhile, bring 4 quarts water to the boil. Put in bamboo shoot, potato and carrot. Boil 5 minutes. Then add cauliflower and boil another 5 minutes. Add cucumber and boil another 2 minutes. Drain in a colander and set aside.

3. At the same time, boil 4 cups of water and cook rice noodles for 5 minutes or until tender. Drain in a colander and rinse in cold water to cool. Set aside.

4. In a large skillet, heat the peanut oil over high heat until it begins to smoke. Sauté the black mushrooms and mushrooms for a few seconds, stirring constantly. Then add all other ingredients except sesame oil, stirring as you add them. Continue cooking in this manner over high heat until the cooking liquid noticeably reduces and thickens. This will happen quite rapidly. Then scoop the entire dish into a serving bowl with a rubber spatula (or a wok scoop if you have one). Toss with the sesame oil and serve.

YIELD: 4 SERVINGS

Cheese Fondue

Fondue is Swiss to the core. It was invented there. It uses the local cheeses. It requires the cooperation of many people, something the Swiss have been good at for centuries, ever since they joined their Alpine cantons into the Helvetic confederation we call Switzerland. Fondue is a meal in itself ideally suited to cold weather and the informality of mountain villages. Its virtues carry over nicely to the American winter and the American temperament (and fit into a vegetarian menu). If, however, you want to do this properly, you will have to acquire a chafing dish, a can of Sterno to heat the dish, some long fondue forks, French-style bread and imported Swiss cheese. American Swiss cheese is too young to melt smoothly, and melting is what fondue is all about. The word comes from the French verb *fondre* (to melt). The fondue cook (perhaps *host* is the more appropriate word) has to strive to keep the smooth pot of fondue from drying out and turning into strings of overcooked cheese or from separating into fat and curd. It's actually quite easy to bring off once you've laid the proper groundwork.

½ pound Swiss Emmentaler, diced
½ pound Swiss Gruyère, diced
3 tablespoons all-purpose flour
1 clove garlic, peeled (see page 43)
2 cups dry white wine
1 tablespoon fresh lemon juice
3 tablespoons kirsch
  Pepper
1 large or 2 small French-style loaves of bread

1. Take the cheese and roll it in the flour in a bowl.

2. Rub the inside of a medium saucepan with the garlic clove. Discard clove.

3. Add wine and set over medium heat. Add lemon juice. Just before the wine reaches the full boil, gradually add the cheese, stirring constantly. Then add kirsch (a clear brandy made from cherries) and pepper to taste, stirring until all the ingredients have melted together.

4. Bring the fondue to the table in a chafing dish. Adjust the heat under the dish so that the fondue barely bubbles, but it must bubble. Guests should be chivied into tearing the bread into bite-size pieces, each of which should have some crust. Each guest must have his or her own fondue fork. The next order of business is to spear a piece of bread with the fork, running the tines through the

soft part of the bread and securing them in the crust. Then, one by one, the diners are to plunge their bread into the fondue, stirring it in the legendary figure-eight pattern. This satisfies tradition and helps to prolong the smoothness of the fondue. The polite fondue consumer does not withdraw his fork until someone is poised to spell him at making figure eights. Also by legend, the first person to drop his bread into the fondue in a restaurant pays for everyone's meal.

YIELD: 4 SERVINGS

Spinach Soufflé

Here is as elegant a vegetable dish as can be imagined. The recipe illustrates the general procedure for a standard soufflé of the type bound together with a béchamel (see page 197) base. It will also show you how to cook spinach for serving as a vegetable by itself. The actual quantity of spinach used for the soufflé is, however, quite small, and this dish is a standard method for using up leftover spinach.

You will probably want to supplement this very rich entrée with bread and a postlude of salad containing solid ingredients such as chick-peas, diced beets (see page 156) or chopped green bell pepper (see page 44).

> 5 tablespoons butter, approximately
> 1 10-ounce package fresh spinach
> Salt
> 1 cup light cream or milk
> 3 tablespoons all-purpose flour
> 4 egg yolks
> 5 egg whites
> ½ cup grated Gruyère cheese

1. Butter the inside of a 6-cup soufflé or charlotte mold. Set aside and preheat oven to 400 degrees.

2. All fresh spinach must be carefully washed in plenty of cold water. Fill the kitchen sink with water. Put in the spinach. Run your hands through the leaves several times to loosen grit. Remove the leaves and put them in a large saucepan with a teaspoon of salt, discarding large stems. Cook over low heat for a few minutes, until the leaves have wilted into a compact mass. There is so much water in and on the spinach that it will cook safely without adding more. In fact, you will have to drain the spinach in a colander and press out excess moisture before serving. Don't overcook the spinach. It should still be a bright green color. Serve as is, or chop it and then serve lightly bound with heavy cream. Salt to taste. For this soufflé, reserve ¼ cup chopped spinach.

2. Stir reserved ¼ cup chopped spinach with 1 tablespoon of butter over medium heat to cook out any remaining moisture. This will take 3 or 4 minutes.

3. Make a béchamel. Set the milk or cream over high heat in a saucepan. As soon as it reaches the boiling point, remove it from heat. While the milk or cream is heating up, melt 3 tablespoons butter over medium heat in a medium skillet. Whisk in the flour and cook, whisking constantly, for 2–3 minutes. Do not brown. Remove from heat. Pour the hot milk or cream directly into the butter-flour roux. Stir thoroughly to blend and remove all lumps.

4. Beat the yolks, one by one, into the hot béchamel.

5. Stir in the spinach.

6. Beat egg whites until stiff but not dry (see page 85). Stir a quarter of the whites into the spinach mixture. Then stir in the cheese. Finally, fold the remaining whites into the spinach mixture (see page 85). Then turn the soufflé mixture into the buttered mold.

7. Place in oven. Reduce temperature setting to 375 degrees. Bake for 25 minutes. The soufflé should rise a couple of inches above the mold and brown nicely on top. Serve immediately.

YIELD: 4–6 SERVINGS

Underground Specialties

As a category of food, root vegetables do not sound appealing. The term conjures up visions of darkness, of dank cold and hairy, pointy, tasteless tubers. This may be why no one says to guests, "We're having root vegetables with the roast." On the other hand, carrots, potatoes and beets are all a part of millions of meals that most people eat happily, even when those roots are just plain boiled. And since it is almost no trouble to rise above the plebeian in this area, you ought to try your hand at preparing these familiar earth dwellers with a touch of class.

Carrots Vichy

This convenient way of boiling carrots automatically provides them with a sauce of butter and a little sugar. The sugar masks the slight natural bitterness of carrots. By legend, the dish originated in the French city of Vichy, infamous as the capital of the French government that collaborated with the German invaders in World War II, but well loved for its mineral water. It is this water, supposedly, in which Vichy carrots were first cooked.

> 1 pound carrots
> 2 tablespoons butter
> ¼ teaspoon salt
> 2 teaspoons sugar
> 1 teaspoon parsley, finely chopped (see page 43)

1. Bring 1½ cups water to a boil in a medium saucepan.
2. Meanwhile, peel the carrots with a vegetable peeler. Cut off the tops and the pointy ends. Then cut into ¼-inch rounds.
3. When the water boils, add 1 tablespoon of the butter, the salt and the sugar. Stir until the butter has melted. Then put in

the carrots. Cook uncovered at a full boil until the water has evaporated. The carrots should be fork tender. If they aren't, add ¼ cup water and boil until it evaporates. No more additions of water should be necessary.

4. Add remaining butter. Stir the carrots in it as it melts. Sprinkle on the parsley and serve.

YIELD: 4 SERVINGS

Mashed Potatoes

As a reporter for *Newsweek* in France in the mid-sixties, I got the plum assignment of covering the award of the third (and highest) star rating in the Michelin Guide to the Auberge de l'Ill in Alsace. My son Michael, then an infant, was at the table, but he wasn't ready to put away foie gras baked in a brioche. The restaurant's owners knew just what to bring: mashed potatoes. But they called them *mousseline,* muslin. Those mashed potatoes deserved their French name, for they were as soft as fine sheets and as white and pure. To get the same result, you must do exactly as I say and avoid blenders and processors, which all too easily turn mashed potatoes to glue.

> 2 pounds potatoes, unpeeled but quartered
> 2 ounces (4 tablespoons) butter
> ½ cup milk
> Salt

1. Put the potatoes in a saucepan. Then add just enough water to cover them. Remove the potatoes. Bring the water to a full boil. Put the potatoes back in and boil until tender, about 20 minutes. It is crucial not to overcook the potatoes. When a fork pierces the largest potato easily, but before the potato softens completely, drain the hot water and peel the potatoes. They will peel very easily, in

strips, if you go after them as soon as they are just cool enough to handle gingerly. You must not let the potatoes cool any more than absolutely necessary, as this would degrade the lightness and smoothness of the eventual puree.

2. Push the peeled potatoes through a potato ricer. This is a commonly available utensil—a perforated cylinder with a press that fits inside it and two arms that force the press against the potato flesh inside the cylinder. Return the pureed potato to a saucepan. Set over low heat and stir while excess water evaporates. Stop heating when a white film begins to build up on the inside of the pan.

3. With a whisk, beat the potato puree vigorously as you add the butter. Continue beating while you bring the milk to a boil in a separate pan. When it boils, beat it into the potato. Add salt to taste and continue beating until the mashed potatoes are very light and almost frothy.

YIELD: 4–6 SERVINGS

Beets

It is truly surprising how few people know how to cook beets, especially considering their versatility. Also, the frugal cook can steam the greens like spinach (see page 204).

> 2 pounds beets
> ½ cup olive oil, approximately
> 3 cloves garlic, forced through a garlic press

1. Trim away greens and reserve for steaming. Put beets in a saucepan and cover with water. Remove beets and bring water to a boil. Return beets to water and cook for ½ hour or until a fork easily pierces the flesh of the largest beet. Drain.

2. As soon as you can handle the beets, rub away the thin layer of outer skin. It should come away easily. So should an undesirable

mushy area of crumbly flesh at the leaf end of the beet.

3. Chop or slice the peeled beets. Serve them hot, as is, or let them cool, dress with the olive oil and serve the garlic puree on the side. Or mix the beets with ½ cup of **mayonnaise** (see page 40).

YIELD: 6–8 SERVINGS

9

FEAST
FOOD

MOST HOLIDAY DISHES CAN BE EATEN ON ANY DAY OF THE YEAR, but they taste better—they resonate in the mind and in the mouth most fully—on the special days we first learned to eat them. The tug of these associations is still strong, even for people whose roots and convictions have been sorely shaken.

Holiday food is also the food that noncooks are most likely to find themselves wanting to cook—and cook well. Almost everybody sooner or later will be entertaining family and friends for Thanksgiving or Christmas. And nothing is worse or more obvious than a botched holiday meal. Everyone is an experienced judge of turkey.

To provide outstanding holiday fare does not require years of watching an older relative. The main trick is to think ahead far enough so that you have assembled special ingredients, extra chairs and plates and flatware and glasses, laid in an appropriate stock of holiday beverages before the liquor stores close, and planned the order of march in the kitchen so that you can have a holiday yourself.

The usual commonsense rules apply. Do dessert baking ahead of time so that the oven is free for the main course. Clean up as much as you can while you work. Be sure you know how much your turkey weighs so that you can time its lengthy roasting to coincide with social reality. Turkey done too late makes the family impatient. Turkey done too soon has to be kept warm while it waits; it dries out and no one will thank you sincerely for cooking it.

A little forethought is really all that is necessary to make a relaxed success out of Thanksgiving, Christmas, Hanukkah, New Year's, Easter, or any other holiday on your calendar. This year, invite everyone to your house.

Thanksgiving

Roast Turkey

This giant native bird has been a symbol of American festivity since 1621, when it was served at the first Thanksgiving. These days, thanks to its adaptability to mass breeding under controlled conditions, the turkey is also a symbol of American skill at efficient production of food. The turkey is, in a word, cheap. But it is also delicious, especially when it is fresh-killed, i.e., not frozen. Almost any market will procure a fresh-killed turkey for you, but you must let them know ahead of time. Inquire well in advance of Thanksgiving and Christmas. You should also calculate the cooking time well in advance, because a very large turkey can take a very long time to roast. For example, a 16-pound bird will take more than 5 hours in the oven, and while it is in there it probably won't leave much room for other foods.

> 1 12-pound fresh-killed turkey
> 1 recipe stuffing (see page 212)

1. Preheat oven to 425 degrees.
2. Spoon stuffing into the turkey's cavity until it is almost full. Then sew up the skin that extends from the cavity. Use a large needle and heavy thread. This is easier than bothering with trussing needles, and easier to disassemble when the bird is done.
3. Put a rack in a roasting pan. Set the turkey on the rack, breast side down. Arrange the oven rack so that the turkey will be centered in the oven space. Slide in the roasting pan with the turkey.
4. Roast for 30 minutes. Then reduce heat to 375 degrees. Roast another 3 hours. Then remove the roasting pan from the oven to a work table or counter. Using a long-handled fork and

potholders, maneuver the bird off the rack, turn it over and put it back on the rack, breast side up. Return to oven and roast approximately ½ hour. During this time the breast skin should brown nicely. Check for doneness by piercing the thigh. Juices should run clear.

By roasting the turkey with the breast side down for most of its cooking time, you have protected the delicate white meat from drying out, the curse of most holiday turkeys. If your turkey is a different size, figure 20 minutes per pound when calculating total oven time.

YIELD: 12–16 SERVINGS

TO CARVE: First sever the legs and thighs at the joints with poultry shears or a knife. Set aside (or better still, have a helper slice off servable slices of dark meat. Two carvers mean faster, hotter service). Then slice the white meat thinly from each side of the breast. Cut off the wings at the joints. Cut off wing tips and discard. Turn turkey over and cut meat from the back as best you can.

Stuffing for Turkey

Stuffings exist to mop up juices and to absorb flavors given off by the turkey as it cooks. Stuffings also contribute flavor of their own to the meal. There are no strict rules, no rigid principles, just a few standard notions about stuffings that people have liked over the years. Once you have tried this recipe, you will probably never repeat it precisely. The basic idea is to take a starch (often bread crumbs) and dress it up with vegetables and seasonings. Inside the bird it cooks into a kind of free-form dumpling. Figure on 1 cup of stuffing per pound of turkey.

¾ pound sausage meat
6 ounces (12 tablespoons) butter
2 ribs celery, chopped
2 medium onions, chopped (see page 39)
 Sage
10 cups bread crumbs

1. Brown the sausage in a skillet over medium heat, stirring occasionally. The sausage should have enough fat to cook in its own juice without adding any additional fat.

2. In another skillet, melt the butter over medium heat and sauté the celery and onion until the onion is translucent.

3. Combine all ingredients, including the sausage fat and butter from sautéing the celery and onion, in a large bowl. Mix thoroughly. If you want a moister stuffing, stir in some water.

YIELD: STUFFING FOR A 12-POUND TURKEY

Cranberry Sauce

Out of the bogs of the Northeast come tart berries unlike any that other countries produce. Whole cranberries store almost indefinitely in the freezer without loss of quality. The traditional Thanksgiving cranberry sauce—an American version of the fruit sauces Europeans serve with game—can be dashed together in 10 minutes and suits pheasant, partridge and venison as well as it does turkey.

1 pound cranberries
2 cups sugar

1. Combine cranberries and sugar with ½ cup water in a saucepan.

2. Bring to a boil, reduce heat until the mixture barely sim-

mers and cook until the cranberries burst. Stir from time to time until this happens, about 10 minutes.

3. Transfer to a serving dish and let cool.

YIELD: 12–16 SERVINGS

VARIATION: Grate the peel of 2 oranges and add to ingredients in step 1.

Candied Sweet Potatoes

Everyone who tries this classic for the first time runs into the same problem. In the chaos that precedes Thanksgiving, he or she discovers that his or her market has no sweet potatoes, only yams. Does it matter? Can you tell the difference? Well, yes, you can tell the difference, because the sweet potato is a more refined vegetable, but the yam is perfectly respectable and more widely available. Almost no one will be the wiser. Many people put marshmallows on top of this dish. I say let them, it's a free country. For my part, I will save my marshmallows for cookouts and children's birthday parties. What follows is an adult version of candied sweets, flavored with the national spirit. The alcohol, for better or worse, evaporates during baking.

> 12 medium sweet potatoes or yams
> 2 cups brown sugar
> 6 tablespoons butter
> ½ cup bourbon

1. Boil the sweet potatoes or yams in water to cover until they just begin to soften. Push a fork into one to test.
2. Drain, peel and slice into ½-inch rounds. Let cool.
3. Preheat oven to 350 degrees. (It is at this point on Thanks-

giving Day that you will give thanks for that second oven you haven't used all year. Without it, you either have to squeeze this dish in with the turkey—if possible—and cook it at a slightly higher than optimal temperature, or you have to wait until the turkey is done and bring the sweet potatoes to the table as an afterthought or else prepare them in advance and reheat at the last minute.)

4. Grease the inside of a large oven-proof casserole. Arrange the sweet potatoes or yams in it.

5. In a saucepan, bring the sugar and ¾ cup water to a boil. Cut butter into mixture. When it melts, stir in bourbon off heat. Then pour mixture over sweet potatoes or yams.

6. Bake, uncovered, for ½ hour or until heated through and tender. Cooking time will vary according to the depth of the sweet potatoes or yams in the casserole.

YIELD: 12 SERVINGS

Pumpkin Pie

Can she bake a pumpkin pie? (Can he?) That is one of the basic tests of kitchen competence in our culture. It is actually quite an easy test to pass and will get you an inordinate amount of praise at Thanksgiving, the classic occasion for this classic presentation of a late-fall vegetable.

   2 cups (1 pound) pumpkin, fresh or canned (unseasoned)
   1 cup sugar
   ½ teaspoon salt
   ¼ teaspoon nutmeg
   2 cups heavy cream
   2 eggs
   1 pie crust in an ungreased deep 9-inch pie pan (page 72)

1. The whole world uses canned pumpkin for its pies. But it is really quite easy to start from scratch if you choose (the end result, however, will not be notably different). When you are cleaning a pumpkin for a Halloween jack-o'-lantern, cut out 1½ cups of the yellow flesh. Then steam it in a covered saucepan until soft. To steam, bring an inch or so of water to a boil in the pan. Set a steaming rack in the water (if you don't have one, a colander will suffice) and put the pumpkin in the rack. Low heat should maintain a steady boil.

2. Mash the cooked pumpkin with a wooden spoon, or puree in a blender or with the steel blade of a processor, or use a food mill or a potato ricer.

3. Preheat oven to 425 degrees.

4. Mix pumpkin together with all other ingredients (except crust) in a bowl. Combine thoroughly. Pour into crust.

5. Bake for 10 minutes. Then reduce oven heat to 300 degrees and bake another 30 minutes or until the filling sets. This is, in fact, a custard pie, which means that it is thickened by the coagulation of egg yolks when they reach a temperature a bit below 200 degrees. It takes the oven a while to raise the entire pumpkin-custard mixture to that temperature. But when it does, the pie sets. The trick is not to overbake the custard, which will then turn grainy. Test with a knife. The filling should be a bit soft at the center and firm but not stiff when you jiggle the pie plate. It will shimmy a little while it is hot, but will stiffen up when it has cooled.

Christmas

Roast Goose

At today's prices, a goose is prodigality itself. But that is the Christmas spirit, after all, giving people luxuries they don't have the rest of the year. And for that purpose, the goose is perfect provender. It is also the traditional bird for the holiday. Tiny Tim Cratchit ate it in Dickens's *A Christmas Carol* and so should you.

> 1 10-pound goose
> 1 recipe potato and sausage stuffing (see page 218)

1. Preheat oven to 375 degrees.
2. Pull any patches of fat from the goose's cavity (they can be rendered—heated until the fat melts—strained and reserved for use in cooking). Stuff goose and sew up cavity (see page 211).
3. Prick the goose all over with a fork so that fat can drain out during roasting.
4. Set on a rack in a roasting pan, breast down, and cook in oven for 1 hour, covered.
5. With potholders and a long-handled fork, turn goose over, prick skin again and return to oven, uncovered. Baste continually with pan drippings. Figure 20 minutes of cooking time per pound (from the time you put the goose in the oven). This goose should take a total of about 3 hours and 20 minutes. It is done when juices from the thigh run clear.

YIELD: 6 SERVINGS

Potato and Sausage Stuffing

The potatoes are ideal for absorbing the richness of the goose drippings. The Italian sausage meat brings with it a mix of seasonings, notably fennel. Potato makes a nice change from the bread crumbs so common in other stuffings.

> 4 medium potatoes
> 3 tablespoons butter
> 3 tablespoons onion, chopped (see page 39)
> ½ pound sweet Italian sausage

1. Boil the potatoes in water to cover for 5 minutes. Peel and dice.

2. Melt the butter over medium heat in a skillet. When the foam subsides, sauté the onion until softened. Meanwhile, cut open the sausages. Scrape the meat into the skillet, stir together with onions and cook until no longer pink.

3. Stir in potato.

YIELD: STUFFING FOR 1 10-POUND GOOSE

Hard Sauce

There is no accepted, fixed recipe for this traditional accompaniment to fruitcake at Christmas. But this hard sauce is as rich and authentic as any, and it will add a homemade touch to dessert. I am assuming you will not attempt to make and age your own fruitcake, since excellent ones are easily bought and there seems to me no shame in purchasing one. Should you decide to plunge ahead and make your own fruitcake, a project beyond the scope of a basic book like this, plan to do it several months before Christmas, because the taste of these brandy-soaked confections definitely improves with time. In any case, hard sauce is the elegant—and standard—finishing touch.

1 cup confectioners' sugar, sifted
1½ sticks (12 tablespoons) unsalted butter, softened
1 teaspoon vanilla
¼ cup heavy cream
¼ teaspoon ground cloves

1. In a mixing bowl, whisk together the sugar and butter until very smooth. This can also be done with an electric mixer.
2. Whisk in remaining ingredients.
3. Chill.

YIELD: ABOUT 2 CUPS

Christmas Cookies

Cookies are a special category of Christmas food. They make excellent projects for children on vacation from school, but busy adults can also enjoy knocking off a batch in a free hour. Cookies make excellent gifts, but you can also just eat them yourself, ending up guilty but also content.

Shaped Cookies

For children and their older relatives, these cookies, which are cut into Santas and stars and other Xmas shapes, are almost as much fun to make as to eat. Every dime store sells cookie cutters and, if you insist, red and green-colored sugar for decoration. The same recipe and method can be put to use on rainy days at any time of the year, although you probably will want to save the Santa cutter for Yuletide.

  ¾ cup sugar
 12 tablespoons (¾ cup) butter, softened
  2 eggs
 ½ teaspoon salt
  1 teaspoon vanilla
 2½ cups all-purpose flour

1. In an electric mixer, beat together the sugar and butter until very smooth. Then beat in eggs, salt and vanilla.

2. Continue beating and add the flour gradually.

3. Wrap dough in wax paper and chill for several hours or overnight. If you don't do this, it will be sticky and hard to roll out.

4. Preheat oven to 350 degrees.

5. Lightly flour a board or counter. With a rolling pin, roll out the dough until it is about ⅛-inch thick.

6. Press cutters into dough to cut shapes. Make the cuts as close together as possible so as to use as much dough as you can. With a metal spatula, transfer cut cookies to an ungreased cookie sheet.

7. Gather up the scraps of dough, consolidate gently into a ball and roll again. Cut additional cookies and put them on the cookie sheet. (You will have to do this in batches, because this recipe produces more cookies than 1 sheet can hold.)

8. Bake 7 or 8 minutes or until golden. Let cool on a rack. Store in a tin in a cool place.

YIELD: 4–5 DOZEN

Walnut Balls

In every recipe file in the Western world, I would bet, there lurks some version of this ultrasimple, rich and foolproof cookie. You can mix the dough in 15 minutes, roll it into little balls, and be done with the baking 20 minutes later.

16 tablespoons (2 sticks or ½ pound) butter, softened
1 cup sifted confectioners' sugar
2¼ cups all-purpose flour
1 teaspoon vanilla extract
½ cup chopped walnuts

1. Preheat oven to 350 degrees.
2. In an electric mixer, beat together the butter and ½ cup sugar until very smooth.
3. Continue beating and add the flour gradually. Then add the vanilla and the nuts.
4. With your hands, roll into balls about the size of robins' eggs.
5. Place on an ungreased cookie sheet and bake for 20 minutes or until golden. Let cool until warm. Then roll in remaining sugar. Store in a tin in a cool place.

YIELD: ABOUT 3 DOZEN COOKIES

New Year's

Eggnog

The classic American holiday drink. I suppose you know this and have imbibed more than a few frothy glasses, ending up with nutmeg freckles on your nose at Christmas or New Year's. Spiked or not, this milk punch will put an official stamp on your winter cocktail table.

> 9 **eggs, separated (see page 41)**
> ½ **cup sugar**
> 1 **cup light rum, optional**
> 4 **cups heavy cream**
> **Grated nutmeg**

1. Using a wire whisk or an electric beater, beat the yolks with the sugar until the mixture turns pale and thick. Then beat in rum, also using a wire whisk or an electric beater. Chill.

2. Wash and dry the whisk (or the electric beater). Now beat the egg whites until they are stiff but not dry. There is a large body of theory you can read about the best way to do this. Purists say that a large wire balloon whisk will force more air into the egg whites than a mechanical beater can manage. Others insist on copper mixing bowls. But excellent results can be achieved with good electric beaters (not with processors or blenders). It is a good exercise to whisk egg whites manually at least once, so that you can see how they change and lighten in the bowl—get the feel of a tricky process in slow motion. An electric mixer makes this happen so quickly, you may miss the magic.

At any rate, you are working toward the nirvana of stiff peaks. The egg whites will gradually change from transparent to opaque to fluffy mounds that hold their shape. Properly beaten egg whites will support an egg in the shell. Just be careful you don't overbeat the whites and dry them out. This usually happens with electric mixers. Hand whiskers are all too eager to quit before they mess things up through excess zeal.

3. Set the beaten egg whites aside. Wash the whisk or beater and whip the cream. Make sure it is fully chilled. It whips much more easily when cold. There is no good reason to do this by hand, although it is certainly within the strength of a normal person. If you overdo whipping cream, you will produce butter, so stop as soon as you have stiff peaks. French cooks stop much sooner, as soon as the beaters leave traces in the cream. This is what the French call the Chantilly stage. If you do not want an extremely stiff eggnog, stop at this point in the whipping of the cream. Stir in the yolk mixture.

4. Spoon the beaten whites onto the whipped-cream mixture. Do not stir them together, which would drive the air completely out of the egg whites. Instead, you must fold the whites into the cream. Use a rubber spatula. Cut with the blade into the center of the whites and down into the bottom of the cream below. Then pull upward and fold over the cream onto the egg whites. Rotate the bowl a quarter turn and repeat. Continue folding and turning until you have combined the whites and cream into a uniform mass. Chill.

5. Just before serving, spoon into glasses or cups. Sprinkle ground nutmeg over each cup or use a whole nutmeg and pull over a nutmeg grater.

YIELD: ABOUT 20 SERVINGS

Yorkshire Pudding

You can, of course, eat this puffy, savory pudding any day of the year—whenever you are also having roast beef. Yorkshire pudding is a lavishly informal combination of beef drippings and an egg-milk batter, very old-fashioned but very festive. It is so festive, in fact, because of the roast that makes it possible, that it makes sense to cook it for a special day. I suggest New Year's.

> 2 cups milk
> 4 eggs
> 2 cups flour
> 1 teaspoon salt
> ½ cup drippings from roast beef (see page 168)

1. The only trick to this dish is timing. It takes about the same time to cook as the roast should have to rest at room temperature before being carved. But you will have to raise the temperature of the oven to 450 degrees immediately after removing the roast unless you have a second oven.

2. Collect the necessary drippings from the roasting pan and reserve. This can be done 15 minutes before the roast is done, if you are using a second oven for the Yorkshire pudding.

3. Warm a lasagne pan or other medium-size baking pan in the oven while it is heating up to 450 degrees. Or, if you are using a second oven, warm the pan during the last 15 minutes of the roast's cooking time.

4. Right after you put the pan in the oven to warm, whisk the milk and eggs together. Then whisk in flour and salt until smooth.

5. Pour drippings over the bottom of the warmed pan. Then pour egg-milk batter on top.

6. Bake 10 minutes. Reduce heat to 350 degrees and bake 15 minutes or until thoroughly browned, but not burned, on top. The pudding should be nicely puffed. Cut it into squares and serve immediately.

YIELD: 8 SERVINGS

Hoppin' John

In Charleston and elsewhere around the South, people eat hoppin' John on New Year's Day. It is named, supposedly, after a crippled black who sold it in the streets of Charleston as far back as 1841. It is a tasty dish, and the rice-legume combination offers complete-protein nourishment even without the ham (or the even more traditional smoked hog jowl that you can substitute for ham if you have some in your larder).

> 2 cups black-eyed peas (or field peas), soaked in water overnight
> ½ pound smoked country ham (or smoked hog jowl)
> Salt
> Pepper
> 1 cup long-grain rice
> Lard

1. Drain peas in a colander. Set in a large pot with the ham. Cover with 8 cups of water. Add salt and pepper to taste and bring to a boil. Reduce heat and simmer until peas are tender, about 1 hour.

2. Remove ham, slice off any excess fat and cut meat into small pieces. Reserve.

3. Drain peas, reserving cooking liquid.

4. Put 1 cup of peas in a pot with the rice along with 2½ cups reserved cooking liquid. Bring to a boil, reduce heat to low, cover and cook until rice is tender, about 15 minutes.

5. Meanwhile, heat 2 tablespoons lard in a skillet and fry ham pieces until crisp. Drain and reserve.

6. On a serving platter, combine pea-rice mixture with remaining cooked peas and moisten with remaining cooking liquid. Place ham on top.

YIELD: 8–10 SERVINGS

Easter

Lamb Shanks Kapama

The high point of lamb consumption in this country every year comes at Easter time, and Greek-Americans account for most of the feasting. Lamb producers understand this, and that means that more and better lamb is available around Easter than at any other season. You could choose this moment to eat **leg of lamb** (see page 169), but why not fall in with the Greek spirit of the holiday as long as you are joining the Greeks in choosing lamb. Lamb shanks kapama is a traditional Greek favorite that exploits an economical cut and makes the most of it with a minimum of fuss. Drink ouzo while the oven does the work.

> 4 **lamb shanks**
> 2 **cloves garlic, finely chopped** (see page 43)
> 1 **large onion, chopped** (see page 39)
> ½ **cup celery, chopped**
> 2 **bay leaves**
> 1 **teaspoon dried oregano**
> 1 **cup tomato paste**
> ½ **cup olive oil**
> ½ **cup dry white wine**

1. Preheat oven to 350 degrees.
2. Put all ingredients in a roasting pan. Add 2 cups water. Stir other ingredients together around lamb. Cover and bake for 1½ hours.
3. Uncover and bake 1 hour or until tender and sauce thickens. Serve with **rice** (see page 183).

YIELD: 4 SERVINGS

Purim

Hamantaschen

These pastries are traditional for the Jewish holiday Purim, which celebrates the heroism of Esther, the Jewish queen who protected her people from the villainy of the powerful courtier Haman by protesting to her husband, King Ahasuerus. *Hamantaschen* are shaped like Haman's trademark, his three-cornered hat. By custom, they are filled either with poppyseeds or with *lekvar* (prune butter). I prefer the poppyseed variety, and that is the recipe I am providing, but if you want to try the prune version, commercial *lekvar*, available at specialty stores, can simply be substituted for the poppyseed filling below. You don't have to be Jewish to love *hamantaschen*.

- ¾ **cup shortening**
- ¾ **cup sugar**
- 3 **eggs**
- 2 **cups all-purpose flour**
- 2 **cups poppyseeds**
- ½ **cup honey**
- 1 **pinch salt**

1. In an electric mixer, beat shortening and ½ cup sugar together until very smooth. Then beat in 1 egg.

2. Take the bowl out of the mixer and continue by hand, beating in the flour and about 3 tablespoons of water. Use a wooden spoon for this. The dough should end up soft and will gather itself into a ball as you work. Now it needs to rest so that it will roll out properly. Chill thoroughly.

3. Meanwhile, prepare the filling. First immerse the poppyseeds in boiling water for 1 or 2 minutes. Then drain them in a fine-mesh strainer.

4. In a saucepan, combine poppyseeds, 1 cup water, honey, salt and remaining ¼ cup sugar. Cook over medium heat, stirring, until thick. Let cool.

5. Beat in the remaining 2 eggs. Then set over low heat and stir until the mixture thickens.

6. Preheat oven to 350 degrees.

7. Roll out dough on a floured board or counter until about ⅛-inch thick. Using an inverted glass, cut out as many circles as you can. Put a walnut-size ball of filling in the center of each. Pull up the edges of the circles to form a triangle. Pinch edges together over the filling to seal it in. Using a flat metal spatula, transfer each *hamantasch* to a cookie sheet greased with shortening (this recipe uses shortening because it is vegetable-based and does not raise problems with religious dietary law, as an animal fat such as butter would).

8. Gather the leftover scraps of dough in a ball and roll out. Repeat step 7.

9. Bake *hamantaschen* for about 10 minutes.

YIELD: ABOUT 2 DOZEN SMALL PASTRIES

Passover

Gefilte Fish

These poached fish dumplings are a fixture of the Passover meal, the high point of food ritual in the Jewish year. Arguments rage over the appropriate combination of fish. This recipe—my wife's version of her mother's—has an outstanding flavor. It is vastly superior to the gefilte fish sold in bottles and can, of course, be served at other times of the year. Grated horseradish is the canonical condiment. The red variety, tinctured with beet juice, makes a nice color contrast to the pale-white fish balls.

> 2 pounds whitefish
> 2 pounds yellow pike
> 1 pound carp
> 3 medium onions, peeled and sliced
> 4 tablespoons salt
> 3 tablespoons sugar
> 3 eggs, lightly beaten
> 2 tablespoons matzo meal
>   Pepper
> 3–4 carrots, scraped and cut into rounds

1. Have your fish man fillet the fish. Take the bones and fish heads with you. And try to get an extra head—it will improve the broth.

2. Grind the fish with 2 of the onions, coarsely, in a meat grinder or processor.

3. Transfer to a wooden bowl and continue chopping with a mezzaluna (a half-moon–shaped chopper) as you work in 2 tablespoons salt, 1 tablespoon sugar, the eggs, the matzo meal and enough water (about ¼ cup) to produce a smooth, light paste. Set aside. If you don't have a mezzaluna, you can do this on a cutting board with a knife. Just make a well in the middle of the mixture when you add the eggs and the water.

4. Put the fish heads and bones as well as the remaining 2 tablespoons salt and 2 tablespoons sugar, pepper, carrots and the remaining onion into a large pot of wide diameter. Cover with plenty of water and bring to a boil. In a separate pot, bring 3 quarts water to a boil.

5. When the first pot comes to a boil, prepare the fish balls. Keeping your hands moist with cold water, form spheres the size of a very large egg (they will expand when cooked) and drop them, one by one, into the pot with the fish bones. The water should be kept at a slow simmer as you continue to add fish balls. When the

paste has been completely used up, continue simmering for 1½ hours. Add additional water from the second pot as necessary, so that there is enough water to keep the balls afloat.

6. Remove from heat and let the fish balls cool in their cooking liquid.

7. With a slotted spoon, remove the balls to a serving platter.

8. Strain the cooking liquid. Pour it into a jar and refrigerate. It should gel. If it doesn't, rewarm the liquid and dissolve a package of gelatin into it. Test by putting a teaspoonful onto a plate and refrigerating. If it doesn't gel, add more gelatin until it does. Refrigerate the liquid.

9. Serve gefilte fish cold, with gelled fish aspic and horseradish.

YIELD: 8–10 SERVINGS

10

AN ESSENTIAL MISCELLANY:

SAUCES, BREADS, PRESERVES AND ICE CREAM

You will get only a taste here of some very large and complicated areas of cooking. But if you get the hang of a few typical sauces, you will easily move on to others in more specialized books. If you learn to bake one basic loaf of bread and want to move on to other kinds, the next steps are easy. The same goes for preserves and ice creams. Get your sea legs here, find out if these special areas of cooking appeal to you, and then you'll know if you want to invest in the appropriate cookbooks and equipment that will help you explore your new-found interests further.

But even knowing how to make one loaf of bread or one kind of jam will greatly expand your options in the kitchen and offer easy ways to prepare edible gifts. In our world, anyone who can bake an honest loaf or bring a hostess his or her own strawberry preserves in a Mason jar with a ribbon tied around the lid soon gets a reputation as a culinary star.

Stocks and Sauces

Classic sauces do not have to be the private preserve of restaurant chefs. Anyone with a 16-quart stockpot, a fine-mesh (chinois) strainer and a freezer can plunge into sauce making of the highest order, practically and economically. Buy the stockpot at a restaurant-supply outlet. The cheapest cast aluminum will suffice. Sixteen quarts is in fact a modestly large pot and will come in handy over and over for sauces and other quantity projects. The recipes here are for the smallest amount that a rational person would consider preparing. They can all be doubled, tripled or quadrupled to achieve significant economies of scale.

Brown Sauce

This is technically a recipe for *jus de veau,* a light, modern brown stock base. Premodern brown stocks were thickened with flour and involved much more physical work. Even this streamlined procedure takes up quite a lot of stove time while the flavor is being extracted from veal bones during long simmering. But remember that you don't have to hover once the ingredients are bubbling away in the pot. And when you are done, you will have liquid gold that can be stored for months in a freezer and quickly melted for use in all the classic brown sauces or simply used by itself as a pellucid, simple sauce for meat.

> 9 pounds veal bones
> 1 pound carrots, peeled and cut into rounds
> ½ pound onions, peeled and sliced
> ¼ cup tomato paste
> 4 bay leaves
> 8 parsley stems
> 4 sprigs fresh thyme *or* 1 teaspoon dried thyme

1. Preheat oven to 400 degrees.

2. Brown the bones in batches in the oven. The idea is to let them take on a caramel color but not to burn. After 15 minutes, start inspecting the bones frequently.

3. Meanwhile, set the stockpot over as many burners as it will straddle and put in the carrot rounds, onion slices, tomato paste, bay leaves, parsley stems and thyme. Add the bones as they finish browning in the oven.

4. Cover pot. Do not add water. Apply high heat for 10 minutes, to sweat the vegetables and get them to yield up their juices. This will not burn the vegetables because the quantity is so large.

5. Pour in a cup of water and continue cooking until it boils away and leaves only a glaze at the bottom of the pan. Repeat this process twice more to produce an intensely flavored and colored stock.

6. Add 5 quarts of water (20 cups) and bring to a full boil, covered. Skim off any scum that rises to the top of the pan with a slotted spoon or skimmer, reduce heat and simmer very slowly for 6 hours, uncovered.

7. Remove all solid ingredients with a slotted spoon or skimmer and discard. Strain through a chinois or other fine-mesh strainer. Cool to room temperature (do not cover the pot while this occurs; a covered pot will encourage the growth of anaerobic bacteria, which will spoil your stock). Refrigerate. The stock will solidify. Then you can easily scrape away the layer of white fat that will have risen to the top.

8. Reheat the stock and bring to a full boil. Continue boiling until you have reduced the volume of the stock to 1 quart. It is convenient to keep transferring the reducing stock to smaller and smaller pans as it reduces.

9. At this point, the stock can be frozen in ice-cube trays. Pop out the frozen cubes and store in the freezer in plastic bags. Then, when you want a small amount of stock for a gravy or sauce or to add distinction to a soup, you can quickly melt down just what you need. If you are serving 8 people, 1 cup of this stock should nicely suffice for a sauce. The classic repertory includes dozens of

variations made by adding special flavorings to the basic sauce. To mention 2: For *sauce diable,* a good sauce for broiled chicken, combine 1½ cups white wine and 2 finely chopped shallots in a saucepan and reduce by ⅔, add ½ cup brown stock, season with Cayenne and serve; for *sauce bordelaise,* a classic with red meat, combine 1 tablespoon finely chopped shallots, 1 cup red wine, 1 crumbled bay leaf, ¼ teaspoon dried thyme and ½ teaspoon salt and reduce by ⅔. Then add 1 cup brown stock, reduce slightly, strain through a chinois or other fine-mesh strainer and serve.

YIELD: 1 QUART

Chicken Stock

In reality, a fine chicken stock can be made with nothing but chicken and water. Take whatever bones and giblets you have and cover them with water. Simmer slowly for 30 minutes to 3 hours (the more time, the more flavor is extracted from the bones), and there you are. In my house, I freeze the giblet package from every chicken I buy. When I have a half-dozen packages, I put them in water and make enough stock for a family soup. (For recipes in this book that use **chicken stock,** see pages 167, 191, 195, 200.)

> Giblets and neck from 6 chickens *or* 2 pounds chicken backs and necks
> 1 chicken carcass (left over from a roast chicken)
> 1 onion, peeled and sliced
> 1 carrot, peeled and cut into rounds
> Salt

1. Put all ingredients except salt in a saucepan. Add water to cover.
2. Bring to a boil, reduce heat and simmer slowly for 1 to 3

hours. If you opt for the longer time, you will probably have to top up the water level every so often.

3. Remove solid ingredients with a slotted spoon or skimmer. Cool to room temperature, uncovered. Chill until the stock solidifies. Scrape away the fat that has collected at the top. It can be saved and used in cooking.

4. Reheat sauce, strain through a fine-mesh strainer or chinois. Cool again, uncovered, and freeze in small containers until needed.

YIELD: 2–3 CUPS CHICKEN STOCK

Tomato Sauce

This is worth making only at the height of the tomato season, when tomatoes are splendid and cheap. Freeze and use later on when good tomatoes are only a bright memory. Substitute in all recipes calling for canned tomato sauce (see page 174), or dilute with milk or cream, to taste, for tomato soup.

> 2 tablespoons oil
> 4 tablespoons butter
> 1 large carrot, peeled and finely chopped
> 1 large onion, finely chopped (see page 39)
> 1 bay leaf, crumbled
> ½ teaspoon dried oregano
> 6 pounds tomatoes, seeded and chopped
> 2 cloves garlic, finely chopped (see page 43)

1. Preheat oven to 300 degrees.

2. Heat the oil and butter in a skillet. Add carrot, onion, bay leaf and oregano. Sauté until onions are translucent. Transfer to a large nonaluminum pot.

3. Add all remaining ingredients, bring to a boil and cook, covered, in oven for 3 hours.

4. Push through a chinois or other fine-mesh strainer. Let cool. Freeze in small containers.

YIELD: ABOUT 1 QUART

Meat Sauce for Pasta

Here is a simple and convenient way to make pasta a full meal. All the ingredients are invariably available in all markets. This sauce tastes better and fresher than bottled sauces, and it contains meat instead of "meat flavor."

> 1 **pound ground beef, preferably chuck**
> 1 **clove garlic, finely chopped (see page 43)**
> 1 **green bell pepper, cored, seeded and chopped (see page 44)**
> 1 **medium onion, chopped (see page 39)**
> 1½ **cups tomato sauce (see page 236)**
> **Salt**
> **Pepper**

1. In a medium skillet, brown the ground beef over medium-high heat. Fat from the meat will be sufficient to do the job without adding more. Just make sure to break up the meat, flatten it and turn it so as to brown all the pieces.

2. Lower heat to medium and stir in the garlic and green pepper. Cover skillet and cook for 10 minutes. Then add onion. Cook uncovered, stirring occasionally, until the onion is softened.

3. Reduce heat to low. Stir in tomato sauce. By the time the tomato sauce has heated through, the green pepper should have completely softened. If not, continue to cook over low heat, stirring occasionally until the pepper is done. Add seasonings to taste. This sauce can be held at a slow simmer for ½ hour if occasionally

stirred. If you have to hold it longer, turn the heat off and reheat over low heat or freeze until needed.

YIELD: SAUCE FOR 1 POUND PASTA,
APPROXIMATELY 4 SERVINGS

Hollandaise Sauce

Hollandaise has a fearsome reputation. It has to be made at the last minute or nearly so (holding it is harder than arranging your life to make it at the last minute). It is technically an emulsion, like mayonnaise (see page 40), in which butter, instead of oil, is suspended in egg yolk to produce a rich, thick and sleek result. However, the butter can curdle out of the egg. And since hollandaise is a hot sauce, the eggs can scramble. But if you are minimally careful and focus on the task, hollandaise is very much within your grasp. It is most frequently served in this country with **eggs Benedict** (see page 105), but it goes beautifully with a very wide variety of foods—fish, broccoli, asparagus.

> 1 **stick unsalted butter**
> ¼ **cup white-wine vinegar**
> ½ **teaspoon salt**
> ¼ **teaspoon white pepper (black will do, but it leaves black specks in the sauce)**
> 2 **large egg yolks**
> ½ **teaspoon freshly squeezed lemon juice**

1. Cut the butter into pats and melt over medium heat in a small, heavy saucepan. Remove from heat. It will cool slightly while you go on to the next step, but it should still be warm when you use it in step 3.

2. In a heavy nonaluminum 1-quart saucepan, combine the vinegar, salt, and pepper. Boil over high heat until only 2 table-

spoons are left. Estimating this reduction will be hard at first unless you are willing to measure once or twice along the way by pouring the liquid into a tablespoon and then into another container. If you still have too much, pour it back into the pan and reduce some more. If you have gone too far, add water to bring it back to 2 tablespoons. The ultimate quantity of the reduction matters, because it will affect the consistency of the sauce and, more important, it will affect the flavor. The purpose of this reduction, besides flavor, is to promote the emulsification of the butter and egg yolks.

3. Whisk the egg yolks into the vinegar reduction, off heat. Then place the saucepan over very low heat and whisk constantly until the mixture has turned pale and visibly thickened. Remove from heat and immediately begin whisking in the melted butter, a drop at a time. After the sauce has clearly taken—in other words, when you are sure that a tablespoon or so of butter has been successfully incorporated and the sauce is smooth and a bit thicker than before—you can whisk in the butter in a steady stream until it has all been added.

4. To make sure that there are no pieces of scrambled yolk in the sauce—and to stop the cooking—pour the sauce through a chinois or other fine-mesh strainer into a warm, clean saucepan.

5. Whisk in the lemon juice. Season with more salt or lemon juice if necessary and serve.

YIELD: 6 SERVINGS

NOTE: You can hold finished hollandaise for a maximum of 2 hours in a double boiler whose water is at, but not higher than, 140 degrees. This is obviously a hard temperature to maintain. If the temperature rises above 140, butter will begin to leak out of the emulsion. You can save the sauce if this happens by whisking a little cold water into it. If the sauce gets too cold, you can whisk in a little hot water. If you do end up holding the sauce in a double boiler—I don't recommend it—don't add the lemon juice until you are ready to serve it, to avoid souring the sauce.

Béarnaise Sauce

Béarnaise is a hot egg-thickened sauce flavored with the herb tarragon. It tastes fresher if made with fresh tarragon leaves, but dried tarragon will get you there. You can also substitute mint leaves for the tarragon, in which case the sauce is called *paloise*. It is a wonderful sauce that suits almost any red meat and will also marry brilliantly with salmon.

As with hollandaise (see page 238), you must proceed with care and steadiness to avoid curdling and scrambling. But since béarnaise is thicker and should be served lukewarm, it is a touch easier to bring off. You can hold it in a sauceboat at room temperature for a few minutes without disaster.

⅓ cup tarragon vinegar *or* white-wine vinegar
½ cup dry white wine
2 tablespoons finely chopped shallots
4 tablespoons fresh tarragon, chopped, *or* 4 teaspoons dried tarragon
½ teaspoon white pepper (black will leave visible specks in the sauce)
3 egg yolks
2 sticks unsalted butter, melted
Salt

1. In a heavy nonaluminum saucepan, bring the vinegar, wine, shallots, 3 tablespoons of the fresh, or 3 teaspoons of the dried, tarragon and the pepper to a boil. Reduce to a bit more than ¼ cup. Measure to be sure you have reduced it enough. Continue reducing if necessary, or add water to compensate if you have over-reduced. Let cool.

2. Whisk the egg yolks into the tarragon reduction. Set over low heat and, whisking constantly, cook until the mixture thickens and turns creamy. Remove from heat immediately.

3. Do not wait. Whisk the butter into the egg-tarragon mixture. Add the butter very gradually and whisk constantly.

4. Strain the sauce through a chinois or other fine-mesh strainer.

5. Take the remaining tarragon and boil it in a tablespoon of water for 1 minute. Drain off the water and whisk the tarragon into the sauce. Add salt if necessary.

YIELD: 6 SERVINGS

Beurre Blanc
(White Butter Sauce)

This is the classic housewife's sauce of the west of France. It is extremely pure in conception—a very small amount of concentrated vinegar causes a large amount of butter to emulsify, thicken and turn silky. The trick is never to let the temperature of the butter rise very far: 100 degrees is the limit. But since you will be starting with ice-cold butter, each pat you add will control the heat of the sauce already in the pan. Just keep at it steadily and you will succeed the first time. Serve with fish, lobster or chicken. Leftover sauce will curdle when it cools. Refrigerate it, and when you are ready to serve, let it soften in the kitchen and then whirl it back together with an electric mixer. Serve cold and let the heat of the food revive it completely.

> 2 tablespoons shallots, finely chopped
> ¼ teaspoon white pepper (black pepper will leave visible specks in the sauce)
> ½ teaspoon salt
> ½ cup white-wine vinegar
> 3 sticks unsalted butter, chilled

1. Bring the shallots, white pepper, salt and vinegar to a boil in a small nonaluminum saucepan. Reduce to about 2 tablespoons. The amount matters. Measure to be sure and continue boiling if

underreduced or add a bit of water to compensate for overreduction.

2. While it is still hot, strain reduction into a clean heavy nonaluminum 4-quart saucepan. Set over very low heat and immediately add 4 pats of butter (about 2 tablespoons). Whisk until melted completely. Then, without pausing, add 4 more pats. Continue until 2 of the sticks of butter have been incorporated. Remove from heat. Then cut the final stick of butter into pats and whisk them into the sauce. Serve immediately.

YIELD: 6 SERVINGS

Shallot Butter

This is one of the so-called *beurres composés*, or compound butters. In the classic French repertory, there is a whole library of these flavored butters. The basic idea is to combine butter and a puree of something else. You then chill the compound butter and serve it with hot food in pats. The heat of the food melts the butter and yields a kind of sauce. The most versatile of these is made from shallots, delicate little relatives of the onion now found in most supermarkets. If you follow the basic method below, you can also substitute 2 teaspoons of chopped fresh parsley (see page 43) for the shallots and produce *maître d'hôtel* butter. Substitute 2 tablespoons of Dijon mustard and you'll have mustard butter. Once you get the hang of it, you can substitute almost any flavoring element and invent your own sauce. All it takes is a blender and a few minutes. Freeze in an airtight bag and use when you need it.

⅔ cup shallots, chopped
1 stick unsalted butter, melted

1. Rinse the blender jar in hot water and dry it.
2. Blanch the shallots in lightly salted simmering water for 3

minutes. Drain shallots in a strainer. Combine with melted butter in the blender jar and puree.

3. Push through a chinois or other fine-mesh strainer. Then transfer to a dish or mold and refrigerate.

YIELD: ABOUT 1¼ CUPS SHALLOT BUTTER

Dill Pickles

Pickling is a gentle form of preservation achieved through soaking food in brine (salted water). Although the process may well be prehistoric and certainly antedates the scientific discoveries that explain how it works, it is fairly complex as chemistry but an easy feat for the cook. You just pour the flavored brine over the raw cucumbers or green tomatoes and let Nature do the rest. And the result greatly overcompensates you for your minimal trouble. As always in home cooking, you control the result, and this means that you can tailor the pickling to your own taste, from crunchy, light-green new dills to half-sours to the venerable, moss-dark, soft but not mushy full-sours in all their dill-and-garlic glory.

It is this last, fully mature stage that large-scale commercial producers never seem to achieve. Their sour pickles are oversoft and undersour. To avoid these pitfalls, you must, first of all, begin with crisp, green cucumbers of medium size or smaller. The Kirby variety, small and nobbly, is ideal.

Next, it is essential to conduct the pickling at room temperature. Pickling is a gentle form of fermentation. The salt in the brine not only draws off juice from the cucumbers, which in itself helps prevent spoilage, but it also promotes bacterial action. The specific salinity (concentration of salt) of the brine used for pickling cucumbers is toxic to most of the bacteria present in the environment that would normally rot the cukes. But it is not high enough to injure certain beneficial bacteria that transform (pickle) the tissue of the cucumbers and stabilize them. In other words, the brine is a bacterial filter that screens out the baddies and lets the goodies make pickles. This process occurs best at room temperature. Refrigeration or the chill of a root cellar will slow it down dramatically (although not totally).

> 30 small-to-medium green cucumbers
> ½ cup coarse kosher salt
> 1 head garlic, sliced
> 1 bunch fresh dill, at least 10 sprigs
> 4 bay leaves
> 10 coriander seeds
> 2 tablespoons vinegar

1. Soak the cucumbers overnight. Drain.

2. While the cucumbers soak, make the brine by bringing 2 quarts of water and the salt to a boil. Let cool. Add garlic, dill, bay leaves, coriander seeds and vinegar.

3. Put the cucumbers in a crock, glass container or enamel mixing bowl large enough to hold them and leave 2 inches of headway. Pour the brine over the cucumbers.

4. Set a plate over the cucumbers and weight it down. This keeps them submerged in the brine. Then spread cheesecloth over the container. This keeps unwanted substances, living and dead, from dropping into your little pickle vat, but permits air to circulate.

5. Let cure at room temperature for a minimum of 5 days. Depending on room temperature and the size and ripeness of the cucumbers, you may want to continue active pickling for as long as 5 weeks. My suggestion is 3 weeks. The deepening color and increasing softness of the cucumbers will help you decide when they are ready, but eventually you will have to cut off a piece of one, taste it and decide where you stand. Remember, they're your pickles.

In the meantime, remove scum from the surface of the brine once a week. And clean the plate before replacing it.

6. When you are happy with your pickles, sterilize enough jars

to hold them (drain the pickles and try loading them into jars, filling each jar about ¾ full). To sterilize, boil the jars in enough water to cover for 15 minutes. Remove with tongs. While still hot, load with pickles. Then pour in enough cold brine to cover the pickles. Seal and refrigerate.

YIELD: 30 PICKLES

NOTE: This same method can be applied to green tomatoes. Most people like dill tomatoes a bit crunchy, so don't pickle quite as long as you would cucumbers.

White Bread

White bread does not have to be Kleenex bread. This standard recipe for a home-baked loaf is fine and white, but it has a crust and a flavor. The method will apply, in general, to all yeast-risen breads. The basic principle is to take dried yeast and encourage it first to come to life in a warm atmosphere and then to feed on the carbohydrates in flour. This process is a kind of natural fermentation that yields carbon dioxide and alcohol. When yeast ferments sprouted barley to make beer, the carbon dioxide escapes and the alcohol remains in the vat. In bread making, properly conducted, only minimal alcohol results (too much will leave a sour, yeasty taste in the bread; sourdough bread gets its name from a modest amount of alcohol) while the carbon-dioxide gas is trapped in the dough.

Wheat flour, and only wheat flour—not rye or any other—contains significant amounts of a potentially elastic protein called gluten, which is activated by kneading and then makes it possible for the moistened flour (dough) to swell and trap air and carbon dioxide. The kneading also distributes the gas in ever finer bubbles throughout the mass of the dough. The more you knead, the finer the bubbles, and, eventually, after baking, the finer the holes in the bread (a well-made bread should have what is called a fine

crumb: small, evenly spaced holes. Commercial bread is so powerfully kneaded, has such a fine crumb, that it is too airy and collapses at the touch, like a tissue). In breads made from nonwheat
flours, the dough is not glutinous—it does not expand elastically
around the gas and allows it to escape into the air. Ergo, nonwheat
bread is flat and dense.

Wheat dough, on the other hand, does trap air and carbon
dioxide as the yeast fermentation gives it off. After a while, usually a couple of hours at a temperature warm enough to promote
yeast activity (ideally, 80 degrees), the carbon dioxide has a bal-
looning effect on the dough. We say that the dough rises, and
indeed a rising dough does seem to have a life of its own, does
seem to be rising of its own accord. Fermentation, once begun,
will continue even in the refrigerator, but it prospers best in a warm
kitchen. Too much heat, however, will kill the yeast. This is what
happens in the oven. As the heat of the oven permeates the dough,
it first accelerates the fermentation and makes the dough rise and
form a loaf in the pan; then it kills the yeast. Meanwhile, the heat
sets the gluten into permanent cells. Despite all this, you do not
have to be a food chemist to bake bread. Just check the expiration
date on the yeast package before you use it and be patient.

1 package dry active yeast
1 cup lukewarm water (about 110 degrees)
  Oil
1 tablespoon sugar
1 teaspoon salt
4 cups all-purpose flour, approximately
1 egg, lightly beaten

1. Combine the yeast and the water in a large bowl. Stir to
moisten yeast thoroughly. Add 1 tablespoon of oil, the sugar and
the salt and mix thoroughly. Let stand for 5 minutes in a warm
kitchen.

2. Stir the flour into the yeast mixture. Soon the mixture will
come together in a mass. It will form a dough.

3. Sprinkle flour on a countertop and turn the dough out onto it. Knead the dough until elastic. This means press and fold the dough with your hands, working it hard against the countertop to activate the gluten and to fold in as much air as you can. In 5 to 10 minutes you will have a smooth mass that feels a bit springy.

4. Wash your hands. Then pour a small amount of oil into a clean bowl and spread it over the inner surface of the bowl with a piece of paper towel.

5. Turn the dough into the bowl. Cover the bowl with a damp towel and leave in a warm, draft-free place for about 2 hours. The dough should by then have doubled in bulk, stretching the gluten as much as possible. One test for this is to poke the dough with your finger. If it mostly stays put and does not spring back to fill the hole, the dough has risen.

6. Flour the counter lightly and turn the dough out onto it. Punch the dough with your fist. It will partly collapse. Now knead it again for a few minutes and then put it back in the oiled bowl. Cover with a damp towel and let rise until it doubles in bulk again. This time 1 hour should be sufficient, perhaps less.

7. Meanwhile, oil a 9 × 5 × 3-inch loaf pan. When the dough has risen properly, punch it down again and form into a loaf shape. Place in the loaf pan, cover with a damp towel and let rise until the top of the dough is level with the top of the pan, roughly 20-30 minutes.

8. During this last rising, preheat oven to 400 degrees.

9. Brush the top of the loaf with the beaten egg. Put loaf pan in oven. Reduce heat to 350 degrees and bake for about 50 minutes or until nicely browned.

10. Remove pan from oven and turn loaf out gently onto a rack. Let cool on its side for 40 minutes before slicing. Oven-hot bread will not be set and may even seem raw when it is not.

YIELD: 1 LOAF

Whole Wheat Bread

Coffee gives this bread its dark color, and a combination of corn-meal and whole-wheat flour gives it its personality. The method is very similar to that used in making **white bread** (see previous recipe), but this way you get two loaves and much credit from friends who admire an honest loaf.

> 2 packages dry active yeast
> 2 cups lukewarm water (about 110 degrees)
> 2½ cups lukewarm coffee
> ½ cup yellow cornmeal
> 9 cups whole-wheat flour, approximately
> 1½ tablespoons salt
> Oil
> Milk

1. Start the yeast in the lukewarm water and coffee (see page 99).

2. In a mixing bowl, combine with cornmeal, whole-wheat flour and salt, knead and let rise twice, as in white bread recipe.

3. After second rising, turn out on a flour-dusted countertop and form into a ball. Cut in half and form each half into a cylinder or a round. Set these loaves on a lightly oiled baking sheet. Leave room between them for expansion. Brush loaf tops with water and let rise for about 20 minutes.

4. Preheat oven to 375 degrees.

5. Brush loaf tops with milk. Bake for 1 hour.

YIELD: 2 SMALL LOAVES

Strawberry Preserves

In this careful but not particularly laborious recipe, a delicate fruit is truly preserved, in flavor and in form, in a smooth strawberry syrup. I could try to fool you and say that this is easy to do well, but it isn't unless you are willing to proceed with care and to weigh the strawberries (at the market or at home on your own scale) and to buy a candy thermometer (the same device that can also be used to verify the high temperatures for deep frying, page 157). Of course, it is possible to make fruit preserves by measuring the fruit and sugar with a measuring cup, but the cup does not measure a crucial variable, the amount of water in the fruit, which will show up when the fruit is weighed. The thermometer eliminates guesswork about the crystalline state of the sugar syrup. For these reasons, I am not going to give volume quantities in this recipe, since I think that would complicate rather than simplify your life and would almost certainly increase your risk of failure.

The quantity specified below strikes me as appropriate, in terms of economy of scale, for one person putting up fruit for one family for one year in one afternoon. But the basic principle is to use equal weights of strawberries and sugar.

> 5 **pounds strawberries**
> 5 **pounds sugar**
> **Approximately 7 small sterilized Mason jars (see page 245)**
> **Paraffin**

1. Cut away the leaves from the strawberries and the little "core" of white to which they are attached. You can do this with either a small knife or inexpensive metal pincers sold in food-gadget shops for this purpose. Don't pile up the fruit as you work. The weight of the berries increases their tendency to squash, already aggravated by storage in crates. Discard any berries that are very ripe or spoiled. Ideally, all berries used for preserves should be firm and, if anything, a touch underripe.

2. Combine sugar with 5 cups water (1 cup per pound) and bring to a boil over medium heat. Once the boil has been reached and the sugar has dissolved, set the thermometer in the dissolved syrup and attach it to the side of the pan with the clip provided for this purpose. Now raise the heat to high and continue cooking until the thermometer passes 235 degrees. (This is the so-called soft-ball stage. It means that the crystalline structure of the syrup has reached a point where if you were to drop some of the syrup into cold water, it would form a pliable ball. Experience shows that after some dilution with fruit juice and a modest amount of additional cooking, soft-ball-stage syrup will cool to a stiff but pourable jelly suitable for preserves. We are cooking it to this point in advance so that it will not be necessary to subject the delicate strawberries to any more than the light cooking necessary to preserve them.)

3. When the syrup reaches the soft-ball stage, spoon in the strawberries as quickly as you can, but try to avoid splashing hot syrup or damaging the berries. Gently lift the berries off the bottom of the pan, where they may have stuck during an initial moment of crystallization on contact with the syrup. Keep the heat high and, after the syrup returns to a full boil, continue cooking until the fruit has begun to look shiny and the syrup has taken on a strawberry color. This should take 5 to 8 minutes of cooking at a full boil.

4. Straightaway, remove the pan from the heat and extract the strawberries from the syrup with a slotted spoon. They should still retain their original shape.

5. Return the syrup to the stove. Bring back to the boil and continue cooking, so as to reduce and thicken to the point where a bit of syrup dribbled on a room-temperature plate will congeal readily. Start testing fairly soon, since you do not want to overdo the reduction and end up with candy. To repeat, the syrup is cooked when a drop of it will congeal on a plate but remain round and swollen in form.

6. Remove the syrup from the stove. Skim off any scum on top of the syrup. Then return the strawberries carefully to the syrup.

7. Spoon into sterilized jars immediately, leaving ½ inch or so of headway at the top. Melt paraffin and pour a small amount into each jar to seal. Screw on lids after the jars have cooled.

YIELD: ABOUT 7 JARS OF PRESERVES

Lemon Ice

The main reason for sorbets and ices is to isolate a flavor, especially a palate-cleansing flavor, and to present it to your sensory apparatus with great force. The cold temperature focuses the taste for you. The most intense of all these very pure cold flavors is lemon.

> 1½ cups sugar
> ¾ cup lemon juice
> 1 tablespoon grated lemon peel

1. Combine the sugar with 1½ cups water in a saucepan and heat until the sugar dissolves. Let cool.
2. Stir the juice and grated peel into the sugar mixture.
3. Freeze in an ice-cream freezer. The ideal consistency is somewhere between slush and fully frozen.

YIELD: 3–4 SERVINGS

Vanilla Ice Cream

This is the classic American ice cream, dating from the early days of the spice trade when vanilla beans entered the country via the Philadelphia docks. It used to be necessary to assemble unwieldy bags of rock salt and ice and then to crank a hand freezer to make one's own ice cream. Now a whole range of electric freezers have eliminated the mess and the strain. You won't save money making your own ice cream, but you will improve on almost any commercial variety. This and the other two ice-cream recipes in this book assume that you have some sort of ice-cream freezer and that it came with its own operating instructions. In all cases, then, put the prepared ice-cream mixture into the machine's metal canister and proceed as directed. If you have no freezer, you can still spread the mixture in ice-cube trays and set them in your refrigerator freezer. After the surface solidifies, stir vigorously and return to the freezer until the desired consistency is reached. If you are going to store the ice cream, transfer it to a covered container before it freezes solid. It is not a good idea to freeze and refreeze ice cream, as this encourages the formation of ice granules.

> 1 cup milk
> ¾ cup sugar
> 2 cups heavy cream (avoid ultrapasteurized cream if at all possible)
> 1 tablespoon vanilla extract

1. Bring the milk to the boil and remove immediately from heat before it foams up and overflows.
2. Stir in sugar until it dissolves. Let cool.
3. Stir in heavy cream and vanilla.
4. Chill 8 to 10 hours, or overnight if possible, to develop flavor.
5. Freeze in an ice-cream freezer.

YIELD: ABOUT 5 CUPS

Mango Ice Cream

The mango is one of the world's great fruits, but it is new enough to American markets so that many people still don't know how to judge a ripe one or how to get at the edible portion. Unripe mangoes taste like turpentine; you definitely want to be sure that the time is right before you cut into one. The best way is to buy fruit when it is still hard and let it mature on your windowsill. It should be noticeably soft but not mushy to the touch. As soon as a black spot appears on the skin, you should cut away the peel. The pit is large and flat. Most of the flesh will cut away in two parcels, attached to either side of the pit. Pureed, it gives a rich, tropical flavor to ice cream.

> 1 cup milk
> ¾ cup sugar
> 1–2 soft, ripe mangoes
> Juice of 1 large lemon
> 2 cups heavy cream (avoid ultrapasteurized cream if possible)

1. Dissolve sugar in milk and let cool as in steps 1 and 2 of previous recipe.

2. Peel mango(es) and cut flesh from the pit. Puree in a blender. Push through a strainer.

3. Stir mango, lemon juice and cream into milk-sugar mixture. Chill 8 to 10 hours, or overnight if possible, to develop flavor.

4. Freeze in an ice-cream freezer.

YIELD: 5 TO 6 CUPS

Index